A SEAL WALKS INTO A CLUB

A SEAL WALKS INTO A CLUB

A side-splitting compilation of the best jokes, gags and one liners

NICK HARRIS

MICHAEL O'MARA BOOKS

First published in Great Britain in 2012 by
Michael O'Mara Books Limited
9 Lion Yard
Tremadoc Road
London SW4 7NQ

A CIP catalogue record for this book is available from the British Library.

Papers used by Michael O'Mara Books Limited are natural, recyclable products made
from wood grown in sustainable forests. The manufacturing processes conform to
the environmental regulations of the country of origin.

ISBN: 978-1-84317-874-3 in paperback print format

1 2 3 4 5 6 7 8 9 10

www.mombooks.com

Cover design by Design 23
Illustration by Andrew Pinder
Designed and typeset by Design 23

Printed and bound by CPI Group (UK) Ltd, Croydon, CR0 4YY

CONTENTS

INTRODUCTION

Just as Lady Gaga is supposed to be the new Madonna, Thursday is the new Friday and brown is the new black, so stand-up comedy has been hailed as the new rock 'n' roll. In these troubled economic times laughter really is the best medicine, particularly when it enables us to take a pop at bankers, politicians and other scourges of modern society. Therefore, hot on the heels of *An Englishman, an Irishman and a Scotsman* and *A Dyslexic Walks Into a Bra...* I have compiled a third compendium of jokes, once again covering everyone's favourite subjects, including bars and blondes, marriage and money, sex and sport. And remember: if you can laugh while everyone around you is looking sad, you probably haven't understood the gravity of the situation.

ANIMALS

An ant and an elephant shared a romantic night together, but the next morning the ant woke to find the elephant dead.

'Damn!' said the ant. 'One night of passion and I spend the rest of my life digging a grave!'

A man bought a donkey from a preacher. The preacher told the man that this donkey had been trained in such a way that the only way to make the donkey go was to say, 'Hallelujah!' and the only way to make the donkey stop was to say, 'Amen!'

The man was pleased with his purchase and immediately climbed on the animal to try out the preacher's instructions. 'Hallelujah!' shouted the man. The donkey began to trot. 'Amen!' shouted the man. The donkey stopped immediately.

'This donkey is great,' he said. 'Just what I need for my long journey.'

And so the man set off on the donkey across plains and mountains. After hours of travel, he realized to his horror that he was heading towards a sheer cliff with a five-hundred-foot drop. In his panic, he forgot the magic word to make the donkey stop. 'Stop!' he cried. 'Halt!' But the donkey just kept on going.

The man tried every word he could think of until, with the donkey getting ever closer to the cliff edge, he said a desperate prayer. 'Please, dear Lord. Please make this donkey stop before I go off the end of this mountain. In the name of Jesus Christ. Amen.'

Hearing the command, the donkey came to an abrupt stop just one step from the edge of the cliff.

The man was so relived he yelled joyously, 'Halleljah!'

A male anteater was rubbing his long snout against the female's snout. Sensing that she was becoming aroused, he whispered seductively, 'Let me kiss you on the lips.'

'Fine,' she said. 'Let me know when you get there.'

Struggling to catch prey now that he had become old and slow, a lion decided he needed a cunning disguise to stop his prey running away from him. So he went into a fancy-dress shop and bought a gorilla suit. He then headed for a watering hole to see if the disguise worked. On the way to the hole, he came across two eagles sitting on a rock.

One eagle said, 'Hi, Mr Lion.'

The other eagle said, 'Where did you get the gorilla suit?'

The lion was devastated. 'How did you know I was a lion?' he asked.

The eagles then started to sing, 'You can't hide your lion eyes…'

Why do gorillas have big nostrils?
 - Because they have big fingers.

A man walked into a bar and ordered a gin for himself and a beer for his dog.

'Sorry,' said the bartender. 'We don't serve dogs.'

'But Rover here is no ordinary dog,' said the man. 'He can talk.'

'Sure,' smiled the bartender. 'I've heard it all before. I bet you're a ventriloquist.'

'No, I'm not,' the man insisted. 'Look, I'm going around the block for a walk and I'll leave you here to talk to Rover. That will prove I'm not a ventriloquist.'

The man disappeared out of the door and Rover turned to the bartender and said, 'Now can I have my drink?'

The bartender was amazed. 'Wow! You really can talk! Will you do me a favour? My wife works in the café next door and it would make her day if you went in and spoke to her. Here's ten dollars to buy a coffee. You can keep the change.'

So the dog took the ten dollars and left. Ten minutes later, the owner returned to the bar and asked where his dog was. The bartender said he was probably in the café next door. The owner went back outside but in the alley between the bar and the café he saw Rover furiously humping a French poodle.

'Rover! What are you doing?' shouted the owner. 'You've never done this before!'

The dog replied, 'I've never had money before!'

John had a first date with a girl who lived on the twenty-third floor of a tower block. As she let him into her apartment, she said, 'I just need to finish getting ready. Why don't you play with Ginger, my dog, while you're waiting? She does wonderful tricks. She'll roll over, shake hands, sit up, and if you make a hoop with your arms, like this, she'll jump right through.'

John casually wandered out on to the balcony to get a view of the surrounding area, and Ginger trotted behind. Just as the girl had said, the dog immediately rolled on its back and offered a paw to shake hands. John thought the dog was delightful, so he made a hoop with his arms and, sure enough, Ginger jumped right through… and over the balcony railing.

Just then the girl appeared on the balcony. 'Isn't Ginger just the cutest, happiest little dog you've ever met?' she smiled.

'To tell the truth,' said John, 'she seemed a bit depressed to me.'

Did you hear about the baby mouse that saw a bat?

– He ran home and told his mother he'd seen an angel.

A man on a golfing holiday was playing the third hole when he noticed a frog sitting next to the green. He thought nothing of it but then just as he was about to play his shot, he heard the frog say, 'Ribbit, nine-iron.' Since the first two holes hadn't gone too well, he decided to follow the frog's advice. So he put away his original choice of club, took out the nine-iron and promptly holed the chip. 'Wow!' he said. 'You must be a lucky frog!'

The frog said, 'Ribbit, lucky frog.'

So the man took the frog with him to the next hole. 'What do you think, frog?' he asked.

'Ribbit, three-wood,' replied the frog. So the man took out his three-wood and promptly sank his tee shot for his first-ever hole-in-one.

'You really are a lucky frog!' the man beamed.

'Ribbit, lucky frog.'

By following the frog's advice on every hole, the man enjoyed his best round ever. To celebrate, he decided to visit a casino that evening and naturally he took the frog along for good luck. Approaching the roulette table, he asked the frog: 'What should I bet on?'

'Ribbit, red fifteen.'

So the man put all his cash on red fifteen, and his number came up. 'You are one amazing frog!' he said.

'Ribbit, lucky frog.'

Collecting his two thousand dollars in winnings, the man decided to book a room in the best hotel in town for the night. While waiting for room service, he sat the frog down on the bed and said, 'Frog, I don't know how to repay you. You've won me all this money and I'm so grateful. Is there anything I can do for you?'

'Ribbit, kiss me,' said the frog.

So the man kissed the frog, and instantly the frog turned into a beautiful nineteen-year-old girl.

'And that, your honour, is how the girl ended up in my room.'

Why did the monkey fall out of the tree?
   - Because he was dead.

Why did the second monkey fall out of the tree?
   - Because he was tied to the first monkey.

Why did the third monkey fall out of the tree?
 - Peer pressure.

Why did the squirrel fall out of the tree?
 - He was doing a monkey impression.

A woman woke one morning to find a ferocious-looking gorilla in the tree on her African plantation. So she phoned the local game warden, who arrived within minutes. In one hand he carried a shotgun; in the other the lead of a fierce hunting dog.

As they walked to the tree, the warden explained, 'I'm going to climb the tree and throw the gorilla out. When the gorilla falls, this dog has been trained to clamp his teeth on the gorilla's genitals and not let go.' The woman nodded but was surprised when the warden handed her the gun.

'What am I supposed to do with this?' she asked.

'Well,' he said, 'gorillas can be tricky to deal with, and it might be that the gorilla throws me out of the tree so that I fall first.'

'And if that happens you want me to shoot the gorilla?'

'No, I want you to shoot the dog.'

Did you hear about the elephant who tried to trace his ancestors on the Internet?

- It was a mammoth task.

An antiques expert was walking along the street when he spotted a mangy old cat drinking milk from a saucer in the doorway of a small, run-down store. As soon as he saw the delicate blue-and-white pattern on the saucer, he knew it was a valuable piece – one that was definitely worth acquiring.

So he walked into the store and said to the owner, 'I'll give you ten bucks for your cat.'

'Sorry,' said the owner. 'The cat isn't for sale.'

'Listen,' persisted the antiques expert, 'I really need a cat around the house to catch mice. I'll tell you what I'll do; I'll pay you twenty dollars for the cat.'

'OK,' agreed the owner. 'It's a deal.' And he handed over the cat.

Disguising it as an afterthought, the expert added, 'Hey, for the twenty dollars, would you mind throwing in that old saucer? The cat's obviously used to it and it would save me having to buy a dish.'

'Sorry, pal,' said the store owner. 'I can't sell that. It's my lucky saucer. So far this month I've sold forty-one cats!'

What do you get if you cross a Frisbee with a cow?
  – Skimmed milk.

A kangaroo kept escaping from his enclosure at the zoo. Knowing that he could hop pretty high, zoo officials put up a ten-foot fence, but the next morning the kangaroo was out again, bounding merrily around the grounds.

So the zoo officials raised the height of the fence to twenty feet, but once again the kangaroo was found the next morning hopping around the zoo.

This continued, night after night, until the fence was sixty feet high. Finally the camel in the next enclosure asked the kangaroo, 'How high do you think they'll go?'

The kangaroo replied, 'Probably a hundred feet unless somebody starts locking the gate at night!'

18

A dog became separated from his master on the African plains. After wandering around lost for a few hours, the dog realized that he was being stalked by a hungry leopard. The dog began to panic but then, thinking on his four feet, he spotted a pile of bones on the ground nearby and began chewing them. Just as the leopard crept up behind him ready to pounce, the dog said in a loud voice, 'Mmmm, that leopard was delicious. I wonder if there are any more around here?'

Hearing this, the leopard turned tail and fled back into the trees, relieved at having had a narrow escape. Meanwhile, a clever monkey, who had been watching the encounter, figured he could put his inside information to good use and gain protection from the leopard. The dog saw the monkey running after the leopard and immediately sensed that the game was up.

Catching up with the leopard, the monkey told him about the dog's deception. Angry at being fooled, the leopard vowed revenge. 'Here,' he said to the monkey, 'jump on my back and see what's going to happen to that conniving canine.'

Seeing the leopard approaching with the monkey on its back, the dog thought, 'What am I going to do?' He considered running, but then decided to sit down with his back to the leopard and pretend that he hadn't seen it. Just when the leopard got close enough to hear, the dog said: 'Now where's that monkey? I can never trust him. I sent him off half an hour ago to bring me another leopard and he's still not back!'

What is a Cat?
• Cats do what they want. • They rarely listen to you. • They're totally unpredictable. • When you want to play, they want to be alone. • When you want to be alone, they want to play. • They expect you to cater to their every whim. • They're moody. • They can really sink their claws into you. • They leave hair everywhere.
Conclusion: Cats are tiny women in little fur coats.

What is a Dog?
• They sprawl all day on the most comfortable piece of furniture. • They hear food prepared a block away but not you in the same room. • They look dumb and lovable all at the same time. • They growl and snarl when unhappy. • When you want to play, they want to play. • When you want solitude, they want to play. • They leave their toys everywhere. • They do disgusting things with their mouths, then want to kiss you. • They go right for your crotch as soon as they meet you.
Conclusion: Dogs are tiny men in little fur coats.

A man walked into a bar and sat down next to a woman who had a small dog at her feet.

'Does your dog bite?' he asked.

'No,' she answered.

But shortly afterwards the dog took a lump out of the man's leg.

The man wailed, 'I thought you said your dog didn't bite!'

The woman said, 'That's not my dog.'

What has horns and a beard and walks through walls?
- Casper the friendly goat.

While visiting a zoo, a man came across an elephant standing with one leg raised in the air. The elephant seemed distressed, so the man approached very carefully. He got down on one knee and inspected the bottom of the elephant's foot, where he found a large thorn deeply embedded. As gently as he could, he removed the thorn and the elephant gingerly put its foot down. The elephant then turned to face the man with what appeared to be a look of deep gratitude before finally walking off. The tourist felt that he and the elephant had really connected in that moment.

The man remembered the incident for years afterwards and wondered whether the elephant's legendary memory worked in the same way. Five years later, the man was walking through the zoo with his son.

As they approached the elephant enclosure, one of the elephants turned and walked over to where they were standing at the rail. It stared at him intently and the man couldn't help wondering if this was the same elephant.

The man climbed tentatively over the railing and made his way into the enclosure. He walked right up to the elephant and stared back in wonder. Suddenly the elephant wrapped its trunk around one of the man's legs and swung him wildly back and forth along the railing, killing him instantly.

So it probably wasn't the same elephant.

A couple new to the neighbourhood hosted a high-society dinner party so that they could get to know the local jet set. As the guests were sipping champagne, the maid quietly informed the hostess that the cat had climbed on to the kitchen table and eaten a large part of the middle section of the salmon that was to form the centrepiece of the first course. The hostess decided to fill the eaten portion with some tinned salmon and hope that with a heavy salad dressing, nobody would notice.

But as the guests tucked into the fish, the maid called the hostess into the kitchen and announced, 'Madam, the cat is dead.'

Seized with panic, the hostess and her husband told their guests what had happened and advised everyone to go to the hospital immediately and have their stomachs pumped. Returning home from the hospital two hours later at the end of what had turned out to be a disastrous evening the hostess poured herself a stiff drink and asked the maid where she had put the cat.

The maid said, 'It's still out on the road where the car ran over it.'

Where do you get virgin wool from?
 - Ugly sheep.

A dog walked into a butcher's shop with a purse strapped around his neck. He walked up to the counter and calmly sat there until it was his turn to be served. Eventually the butcher leaned over the counter and asked the dog what it wanted today. The dog put its paw on the glass case in front of the ground beef, and the butcher said, 'How many pounds?'

The dog barked twice, so the butcher made a package of two pounds of ground beef. He then said, 'Anything else?' The dog pointed to the pork chops, and the butcher said, 'How many?' The dog barked four times, and the butcher made up a package of four pork chops.

The dog then walked round behind the counter so the butcher could get at the purse. The butcher took out the appropriate amount of money and tied two packages of meat around the dog's neck.

Another customer, who had been watching all this, decided to follow the dog. It walked for several blocks and then went up to a house where it began to scratch the door to be let in. As the owner opened the door, the customer said to the owner, 'That's a really smart dog you have there.'

'He's not really that smart,' said the owner. 'This is the second time this week he's forgotten his key.'

Your Cat Owns You If...
• You sleep in the same awkward position all night because it annoys your cat when you move.
• You select your friends based on whether your cat likes them.
• You watch bad TV shows because your cat is sleeping on the remote.
• You have ever worn a pair of slippers with a furball in them.
• You buy more than fifty pounds of cat litter a month.
• You have ever spent half an hour happily playing with a toy mouse.
• You let your cat sleep on your head.
• You let your cat lick your dinner plate clean... while you're still eating from it.
• You have more than four opened but rejected cans of cat food in the refrigerator.

Three creatures were arguing about who was the best. The first, a hawk, maintained that he was the best because he had great eyesight, could fly at speed and swoop on his prey from tremendous heights.

The second, a lion, insisted he was the best because he was so strong that no other animal in the jungle would dare challenge him.

The third, a skunk, pointed out that he needed neither the power of flight nor brute strength to see off a predator.

As the three continued to debate the issue, a huge grizzly bear came along and swallowed them all: hawk, lion, and stinker.

Did you hear about the man who named his dogs Rolex and Timex because they were watch dogs?

A newly discovered chapter in the Book of Genesis has finally provided the answer to the eternal question: 'Where do pets come from?'

Adam said, 'Lord, when I was in the garden, you walked with me every day. Now I no longer see you. I am lonely here and it is difficult for me to remember how much you love me.'

And God said, 'No problem! I will create a companion for you who will be with you for ever and who will be a reflection of my love for you, so that you will love me even when you cannot see me. Regardless of how selfish, childish or unlovable you may be, this new companion will accept you as you are and will love you as I do, in spite of yourself.'

And God created a new animal to be a companion for Adam. And it was a good animal. And God was pleased. And the new animal was pleased to be with Adam and he wagged his tail. And Adam said, 'Lord, I have already named all the animals in the kingdom and I cannot think of a new name for this animal.'

And God said, 'No problem, because I have created this new animal to be a reflection of my love for you. Therefore, his name will be a reflection of my own name, and I will call him Dog.'

And Dog lived with Adam and was a companion to him and loved him.

And Adam was comforted.

And God was pleased.

And Dog was content and wagged his tail.

Soon it came to pass that Adam's guardian angel came to the Lord and said, 'Lord, Adam has become filled with pride. He struts and preens like a peacock and believes he is worthy of adoration. Dog has indeed taught him that he is loved, but perhaps too well.'

And the Lord said, 'No problem! I will create for him a companion who will be with him for ever and who will see him as he is. The companion will remind him of his limitations, so he will know that he is not always worthy of adoration.'

And so it came to pass that God created Cat to be a companion to Adam.

And Cat would not obey Adam.

And when Adam gazed into Cat's eyes, he was reminded that he was not the Supreme Being. And Adam learned humility.

And God was pleased.

And Adam was pleased.

And Dog was pleased.

And Cat didn't give a damn one way or the other.

What's green, black and white?
- A frog sitting on a wet newspaper.

What kind of shoes do frogs wear?
- Open-toed.

A humble crab fell in love with a beautiful lobster princess, but her father, the king, forbade the relationship on the grounds that the crab was of lowly stock.

The unsuitable suitor was a crushed crustacean. 'Why does your father disapprove of me so?' he wailed.

The princess replied tearfully, 'Daddy says you're not a well-dressed crab, but in truth, he doesn't care much for crabs anyway. He says they're common and, above all, they have that silly sideways walk. I'm so sorry, my darling, but it appears that we can never be together.'

The crab was determined to prove the king wrong and win the claw of his fair daughter. The perfect opportunity to prove his worth was the forthcoming Grand Lobster Ball, an occasion that attracted lobsters from far and wide to feast, drink and dance. While the king sat on his throne, the lobster princess sat sombrely at his side, her heart longing for her absent lover.

Suddenly the huge double wooden doors flew open and in walked the crab. The music stopped and all eyes focused on him as he painstakingly made his way up the red carpet towards the throne, walking dead straight, one claw after another. Nobody had ever seen a crab walk straight before. Even the king was impressed.

Finally, after fifteen minutes of straight walking, the crab reached the throne. There, he stopped, looked up at the king and said, 'God, I'm drunk!'

How To Tell the Weather
Go to your back door and look for the dog. If the dog is

at the door and he is wet, it's probably raining. But if the dog is standing there really soaking wet, it is probably raining really hard. If the dog's fur looks like it's been rubbed the wrong way, it's probably windy. If the dog has snow on his back, it's probably snowing. Of course, to be able to tell the weather like this, you have to leave the dog outside all the time, especially if you expect bad weather.

Yours sincerely, the cat.

ARMY, NAVY AND AIR FORCE

Attempting to sneak back on board ship at three o'clock in the morning following a heavy drinking session ashore, a sailor was dismayed to find the chief petty officer waiting for him. With the sailor unable to provide a good excuse for being late, he was issued with an immediate punishment. 'Take this broom,' ordered the CPO, 'and sweep every link on this anchor chain by daybreak.'

The sailor picked up the broom and started to sweep but as he did so, a tern landed on the broom handle. The sailor gestured at the sea bird to leave, but it refused to move. So he picked the tern off the broom handle and tossed it out of the way. However, a few minutes later, the tern returned, once again alighting on the broom handle, and again the sailor was obliged to toss the bird overboard.

This battle of wills continued throughout the night. Each time the tern landed on the broom handle, the sailor tossed it aside, only for it to come back a couple of minutes later. He was so distracted by the bird that he was unable to get much cleaning done as he could only sweep at the chain's links once or twice before the bird reappeared.

As dawn broke, the CPO arrived to check up on the sailor's progress. He was not impressed. 'What have you been doing all night?' he barked. 'This chain is no cleaner than when you started! What's your explanation?'

'I'm sorry,' said the sailor, 'but I tossed a tern all night and couldn't sweep a link.'

A knight in medieval England returned with his men to the king's castle bearing bags of gold and half a dozen slave women, the fruits of plundering the land for seven days.

'Where have you been all this time, Sir Athelmane?' asked the king.

'I have been robbing and pillaging on your behalf all week, sire, burning the villages of your enemies in the north.'

'But I don't have any enemies in the north,' protested the king.

'You have now, sire.'

A platoon of soldiers had been stranded in the desert for a month and supplies were running low. With no imminent hope of rescue, the platoon commander ordered a handful of men to set off in search of alternative foodstuffs.

Two days later, the men returned. 'We've got good news and bad news,' said one of the soldiers.

'What's the bad news?' asked the commander.

'All we found to eat is camel sh*t,' replied the soldier.

'And the good news?'

'There's tons of the stuff!'

Two sailors on shore leave were walking down the street when they noticed a beautiful blonde.

The first sailor asked his friend, 'Have you ever slept with a blonde?'

'Yes, I have,' said the second sailor.

A little further on, they spotted a gorgeous brunette.

'Have you ever slept with a brunette?' asked the first sailor.

'Yes, I have,' said the second sailor.

A few hundred yards further on, they saw a stunning redhead.

'Have you ever slept with a redhead, then?' asked the first sailor.

'Not a wink,' smiled his friend.

On a week's leave from the RAF during World War Two, a young airman decided to grow a moustache. On his first morning back at the base, his warrant officer barked, 'Jenkins, what's so special about your nose that you think it has to be underlined?'

As the whole family sat around the dinner table, the youngest son suddenly announced that he had just signed up at an army recruitment office. For a second or two there was stunned silence, followed by laughter as his older brothers expressed their disbelief that he could handle army life.

'You haven't really signed up, have you?' said one.

'You'd never get through basic training,' scoffed another.

Even his father was sceptical. 'It's going to take a lot of discipline, son. Are you sure you're ready for that?'

Under fire from all sides, the new recruit turned in desperation to his mother for support. But she said simply, 'Are you really going to make your own bed every morning?'

A young ensign had nearly completed his first overseas tour of sea duty when he was given an opportunity to display his ability at getting the ship under way. With a stream of crisp commands, he had the decks buzzing with men and soon the ship had left port and was streaming out of the channel. The ensign's efficiency was remarkable. In fact, the deck was abuzz with talk that he had set a new record for getting a destroyer under way.

The ensign glowed at his accomplishment and was not at all surprised when another seaman approached him with a message from the captain. He was, however, a bit surprised to find that it was a radio message, and he was even more surprised when he read: 'My personal congratulations upon completing your preparation exercise according to the book and with amazing speed. In your haste, however, you have overlooked one of the unwritten rules – make sure the captain is aboard before getting under way.'

In the course of an army war game a commanding officer's jeep got stuck in the mud. The CO saw some men idling around and asked them to help him get unstuck.

'Sorry, sir,' said one of the loafers, 'but we've been classified dead and the referee said we're not allowed to contribute in any way.'

The quick-thinking CO then turned to his driver and said, 'Go and drag a couple of those dead bodies over here and throw them under the wheels to give us some traction.'

Riding through the forest one day, a medieval duke noticed a number of archery targets on trees with an arrow right in the centre of each one. Impressed by such magnificent marksmanship, the duke instructed his followers to find the archer responsible so that he could recruit the man for his private army. Later that day, they returned with a small boy who was carrying a bow and arrow.

The duke could scarcely believe his eyes. 'Do you mean to tell me that this mere boy is the master archer?'

'Yes, sire, it is me,' said the boy.

The duke looked at him suspiciously. 'Are you sure you didn't just walk up to the targets and then hammer arrows in the centre?'

'No, sire,' replied the boy. 'I swear on my mother's life that I shot the arrows from one hundred paces.'

'Very well,' said the duke, 'I believe you and hereby admit you into my service on an annual salary of fifty gold sovereigns for the next ten years. Is that acceptable to you?'

'Yes, sire,' answered the boy. 'It is most generous of you.'

The duke patted the boy on the head and said with a smile, 'But you must tell me how you came to be such an outstanding shot.'

'It's not difficult, sire,' said the boy. 'First, I fire the arrow at the tree, and then I paint the target around it.'

Soon after being transferred to a new duty station, a Marine called home to tell his wife he would be late. He went on to say that dirty magazines had been discovered in the platoon's quarters and they had to police the area.

The wife said, 'Quite right, too! Those publications are seedy and demeaning to women.'

'No, honey,' explained the husband. 'Dirty magazines means the clips from their rifles had not been properly cleaned.'

For a large function in the officers' mess at an RAF camp, the guard at the entrance barrier was a young airman who had only recently been posted there. Aware that the airman was unfamiliar with most of the personnel, his sergeant ordered him to be extra vigilant and not to let any vehicle pass through the barrier unless it had a special sticker on the windscreen.

All went smoothly until a staff car drew up with an air vice-marshal sitting in the back.

'Halt! Who goes there?' barked the young airman, adhering strictly to the procedure.

'Air Vice-Marshal Whittington-Smythe,' replied the corporal driver.

'I'm sorry, I can't let you through,' said the airman. 'You don't have a special pass on your windscreen.'

'Absolute poppycock!' thundered the air vice-marshal in the back seat. 'Carry on, driver!'

'You can't,' argued the guard. 'I have orders to shoot anyone who tries to get in without a pass.'

The impatient air vice-marshal repeated his order to drive on, at which point the young airman went up to the car's open window and said to the AVM, 'Excuse me, sir, but I'm new to this sort of thing. Do I shoot you or the driver?'

A new young recruit arrived at a Foreign Legion post in the middle of the desert. He asked his corporal what the men did for recreation.

'You'll see,' replied the corporal, smiling.

'But,' said the young recruit, 'there are a hundred men at this base and no women. How do you survive?'

'You'll see,' the corporal repeated.

That afternoon, three hundred camels were herded

into the corral, and all the men immediately rushed over to them excitedly chanting, 'Sex! Sex! Sex!'

The young recruit saw the corporal hurrying past and said to him, 'Oh, I see what you meant now, but I don't understand why everyone's in such a hurry. There must be three times as many camels as men.'

'Well,' said the corporal, 'you don't want to end up with an ugly one!'

ART AND BOOKS

A couple went to an art gallery. They found a picture of a naked woman whose private parts were covered by leaves. The wife didn't like it and moved on but the husband kept looking at the picture.

After a few minutes, the wife asked, 'What are you waiting for?'

The husband replied: 'Autumn.'

What's the definition of a modern artist?
- Someone who throws paint on a canvas, wipes it off with a cloth and sells the cloth.

Did you hear about the book on cowardice?
- It had no spine.

Did you hear about the book on copyright infringement?
- It had legal binding.

Did you hear about the book on fashion?
- It had a smart jacket.

Did you hear about the new Chinese cookbook?
- *101 Ways To Wok Your Dog.*

A father and his son were looking at a Nativity painting in an art gallery – it was Titian's world-famous depiction of the scene at Bethlehem. The boy asked, 'Why is the baby lying in such a cheap cradle in a pile of straw?

His father explained, 'Because they were a very poor family and couldn't afford anything better.'

'Well then,' said the boy, 'how come they could afford to have their picture painted by such an expensive artist?'

After his wife divorced him, Tom asked his artist friend Henry to fix him up with a blind date. Henry obliged, but the next day Tom phoned him angrily. 'That woman you lined me up with last night was hideous,' raged Tom. 'She was cross-eyed, nearly bald, had a long twisted nose, a lopsided chest and her ankles were thicker than her thighs.'

Henry replied, 'I guess either you like Picasso or you don't.'

Batty Books
- *The Haunted House* by Hugo First
- *Leo Tolstoy* by Warren Peace
- *Dash to the Loo* by Will E. Makit (illustrated by Betty Wont)
- *Diet for Dogs* by Nora Bone
- *Fitting Carpets* by Walter Wall
- *Dentistry for Beginners* by Phil McCavity
- *A History of Rag and Bone Men* by Orson Cart
- *Aches and Pains* by Arthur Ritis
- *The Russian With Three Testicles* by Ooja Nikobolokov
- *Show Jumping* by Jim Carner
- *Reading Difficulties* by Liz Dexia
- *The Unhappy Customer* by Mona Lott

- *I Nearly Missed the Bus* by Justin Time
- *The Bumper Book of Welsh Jokes* by Dai Laffin
- *Don't Give Up* by Percy Vere
- *Robots* by Anne Droid
- *The Worst Weekend of My Life* by Helen Back
- *Drop Your Knickers* by Lucy Lastic
- *End of the Week* by Gladys Friday
- *House Construction* by Bill Jerome Holm

BANKERS

A young banker decided to buy his first tailor-made suit. So he went to the finest tailor in town to be measured up. The following week, he went in for the first fitting but while admiring himself in the mirror he was dismayed to find the suit had no pockets.

He mentioned this to the tailor, who said, 'Didn't you tell me you were a banker?'

'Yes, I did.'

'Well,' said the tailor, 'whoever heard of a banker with his hands in his own pockets?'

A priest, a doctor and a banker were shipwrecked on a desert island. They could see the mainland in the distance and realized that their only hope of survival was to swim for it. However, they were aware that the island was circled by huge man-eating sharks.

Eventually, the priest said, 'God will protect me, so I will swim to the mainland and fetch help.'

While the doctor and banker distracted the sharks, the brave priest swam as fast as he could towards the mainland, but just fifty yards from his goal, a shark snatched him from behind and ate him.

When the doctor and banker saw what had happened, the doctor said, 'I was a swimming champion at school. If you distract the sharks, I will try to swim to the mainland to save us.'

So the banker distracted the sharks by jumping up and down on the island, allowing the doctor to swim towards the mainland. But just a few yards from shore, a shark grabbed him by the legs and ate him.

Left alone, the banker knew that he must somehow try to swim to the mainland even though he was a weak swimmer. So he set off and when he was just a few yards from the mainland, a shark suddenly grabbed his exhausted body and lifted him safely into shallow water before releasing him unharmed.

Amazed at his lucky escape, the banker said to the

shark, 'The priest was a man of God, yet you ate him. The doctor saved people's lives, yet you ate him too. Why did you save me – a banker – from drowning and carry me to shore?'

The shark replied, 'Professional courtesy.'

What do you call ten bankers buried up to their necks in the sand?

   – Football practice.

What's the difference between a banker and a bucket of manure?

   – The bucket.

A little old lady tried to phone her local bank but was put through instead to the bank's call centre in India.

'Is that the High Street branch?' she asked.

'No, madam,' replied the voice at the other end. 'It is now company policy to deal with all telephone calls centrally.'

'Well, I really need to speak to the branch,' said the old lady.

'Madam, if you just let me know your query, I'm sure I can help you.'

'I don't think you can, young man. I need to speak to the branch.'

The call centre operator was adamant. 'There's nothing that the branch can help you with that can't be dealt with by me.'

'Very well then,' sighed the old lady. 'Can you just check on the counter? Did I leave my gloves behind when I came in this morning?'

How do you save a banker from drowning?
  - Shoot him before he hits the water.

A young man was introduced to a girl at a party and immediately started paying her outrageous compliments and telling her that he hoped this would be the start of a beautiful relationship. He was such a fast mover that within just twenty-five minutes of meeting her, he was proposing marriage.

'Hold on,' she said, taken aback by the speed of it all. 'We met less than half an hour ago. How can you be so sure that I'm the one for you? We hardly know each other.'

'Oh, I'm absolutely sure you're the girl for me,' he said. 'You see, for the past five years I've been working in the bank where your father has his account.'

Albert Einstein died and went to Heaven, only to be informed that his private room was not yet ready and that in the meantime he would have to share a dormitory. Einstein was perfectly happy with this arrangement and looked forward to meeting his new roommates.

'Mr Einstein,' said the doorman, 'this is your first roommate. He has an IQ of one hundred and eighty.'

'That's great,' said Einstein. 'We can discuss mathematics.'

'And here is your second roommate,' continued the doorman. 'His IQ is one hundred and fifty.'

'That's wonderful,' said Einstein. 'We can discuss physics.'

'And this is your third roommate. His IQ is one hundred.'

'Wonderful,' said Einstein. 'We can discuss the latest plays at the theatre.'

Just then another man stepped forward to shake Einstein's hand. 'I'm your last roommate, but I'm sorry my IQ is only sixty.'

'Not a problem,' said Einstein with a smile. 'So tell me, which way do you think interest rates are heading?'

BARS

A man walked into a bar and said to the bartender, 'Give me a beer before the arguments start.'

The bartender poured him a beer.

A couple of minutes later, the man said again, 'Give me a beer before the arguments start.'

The bartender poured him another beer.

A few minutes later, the man said for a third time, 'Give me a beer before the arguments start.'

Totally confused, the bartender said, 'Listen, when are you going to pay for all these beers?'

The man sighed. 'Now the arguments start.'

A cowboy rode into town and stopped at a saloon for a drink. But the locals didn't take kindly to strangers like him and when he finished his drink he found that his horse had been stolen. So he went back into the saloon, fired a shot into the ceiling and yelled, 'Which one of you sidewinders stole my horse?'

Nobody answered. 'Have it your way,' said the cowboy menacingly, 'but if my horse ain't back by the time I've finished this next beer, I'm gonna have to do what I did in Wyoming. And believe me, I don't wanna do what I had to do in Wyoming.'

The locals began to shift nervously in their seats. The cowboy finished his beer, walked outside and saw that his horse had been returned to its post. He then climbed into the saddle and prepared to ride out of town. Just as the cowboy was about to set off, the bartender came out and said, 'Hey, mister, before you go, what happened in Wyoming?'

The cowboy replied, 'I had to walk home.'

A man walked into a bar and ordered a beer. The bartender looked at him and asked, 'Have you seen Eileen?'

The man was confused and said, 'Eileen who?'

The bartender laughed. 'I lean over and you kiss my butt!'

The man was so offended by this that he walked out and went into the bar across the street. While drinking his beer there, he told the bartender what the other barman had said to him. 'This is what you should do,' said the second bartender. You should go back over there and ask him if he has seen Ben, and when he says, "Ben who?" you say, "I bend over and you kiss my butt."'

So the man went back across the street and asked the bartender if he had seen Ben.

'Yeah,' said the bartender, 'he just went out the door with Eileen.'

The man asked, 'Eileen who?'

Once upon a time, this guy named Seth decided that he was rough and tough enough to seek his fortune in the Wild West. So he made his way to a frontier town and became the bartender at the wildest saloon in the territory. He soon proved how rough and tough he was, and the owner of the bar was pleased with how he broke up fights and didn't skim off the receipts. The owner praised Seth for doing a fine job, but added he should remember one thing: 'If you ever hear even a rumour that Mad Martin is coming to town, just save what you can, put a bottle of Red Eye on the counter and head out of town as fast as you can.'

Seth was eager to find out more about this guy, and on making enquiries among the locals was told that Mad Martin was an old mountain man who lived up in the hills and only came to town once or twice a year. However, Martin was the most dangerous guy they had ever heard of and few had ever encountered him and lived to tell the tale. Seth was intrigued.

Then one day a few months later, a cowboy came riding through town at full speed, yelling, 'Mad Martin's coming! Head for the hills!' Everybody in town immediately jumped on their horses and took off for the hills – all, that is, except Seth. He wanted to see this guy because he didn't believe he could be all that tough. So Seth just put the bottle of Red Eye on the bar, hid behind the counter and waited.

He didn't have long to wait. Soon there was a noise in the street. As Seth looked out through a hole in the wall, he saw this huge, mean-looking guy riding down the centre of the street on the biggest bull buffalo that Seth had ever seen. The guy stopped the buffalo in front of the bar, jumped off the beast, punched it in the head (dropping the critter to its knees) and bellowed, 'Wait here till I get back!' He then turned and stomped up the steps. Seth saw that the guy had a pair of huge mountain lions on leashes. He tied them both to a post and kicked them soundly, hollering, 'You pussycats stay here till I'm done!' The cats fearfully sat down.

Into the bar stormed the colossus, ripping the doors off the wall as he passed. With two strides he approached the bar, picked up the bottle of Red Eye, bit off the neck and downed it all in one gulp. Terrified by now, Seth let out a little whimper. The guy looked down over the bar and roared, 'What the hell do you think you're looking at!?'

'N... n... n... nothing, mister,' stammered Seth nervously. 'Do you want another bottle of Red Eye?'

'Hell, no!' said the guy. 'I don't have time! I gotta get out of here – Mad Martin's coming!'

A number twelve walked into a bar and asked for a drink. 'Sorry, I can't serve you,' said the bartender.

'Why not?' asked the number twelve indignantly.

'Because you're under eighteen.'

A man sat down at a bar and ordered a beer. After finishing his drink, he peeked inside his jacket pocket and then ordered another beer. Once he had finished that, he again peeked inside his jacket pocket before ordering another beer.

This went on for six beers until finally the bartender asked him, 'Why do you keep looking inside your jacket pocket before you order another drink?'

The man said, 'I'm peeking at a photo of my wife. When she starts to look good, I know it's time to go home.'

A man sat down at a bar next to an attractive woman. He glanced at her, and then casually looked at his watch.

Noticing this, the woman asked, 'Is your date late?'

'No,' he replied. 'I recently got this state-of-the-art watch and I was just testing it.'

'What's so special about it?' asked the woman.

'It uses alpha waves to talk to me telepathically.'

'What's it telling you now?'

'It says you're not wearing any panties.'

The woman giggled and said, 'Well, it must be broken because I am wearing panties.'

The man smiled, tapped his watch and said, 'Damn thing's an hour fast!'

A businessman travelling through rural England decided to stop the night at a pretty country inn, the George and Dragon. Checking in at reception, he asked the lady co-owner whether meals were still being served at the bar.

'No,' she replied forcefully. 'Last meals are 8 p.m. sharp. It is now 8.13 p.m.'

'Not even a sandwich?' he asked sheepishly.

'No, not even a sandwich. The chef has packed up, and I'm certainly not going to start slaving away in the kitchen at this time of night just because you haven't planned your itinerary very well.'

'OK,' he said wearily. 'Is there any chance of having breakfast in my room in the morning?'

'Certainly not,' she snapped. 'All breakfasts are served in the dining room at 7.30 a.m. prompt. Any more questions?'

'Yes. Do you think I might have a word with George?'

A brain walked into a bar and ordered a beer. The barman said, 'I can't serve you.'

'Why not?' asked the brain.

The barman said: 'Because you're already out of your head.'

BATTLE OF THE SEXES

Eyeing up a young woman who worked in the same office, a man said, 'Nice sweater. Is it made of camel fabric?'

'What makes you think that?' she asked.

'Because of the two bumps,' he grinned.

Concealing her indignation, she replied, 'And your leather jacket, that must be made of pig leather?'

'Why?' he queried.

'Because the head is still on it.'

A young man took a girl out on their first date, to see a movie. A few minutes into the movie, he asked her, 'Can you see OK there?'

'Yes,' she answered, 'I can see fine, thanks.'

A few seconds later, he asked, 'Is your seat comfortable?'

'Yes,' she replied, 'it's very comfortable, thanks.'

'You're not in a draught, are you?'

'No,' she said, impressed by his attentiveness, 'I can't feel a draught at all.'

'Good,' he said. 'Let's swap seats.'

A husband was trying to prove to his wife that women talk more than men. He showed her a study which indicated that whereas men use around 10,000 words a day, women use 20,000.

His wife thought about this for a while and then said, 'The reason women use twice as many words as men is because we have to repeat everything we say.'

Her husband looked at her incredulously and said, 'What?'

What's the best way to get a youthful figure?
- Ask a woman her age.

A woman didn't come home one night. The next morning she told her husband that she had slept over at a friend's house. The husband called his wife's ten best friends. None of them knew anything about it.

A man didn't come home one night. The next morning he told his wife that he had slept over at a friend's house. The wife called her husband's ten best friends. Eight of them confirmed that he had slept over and two said he was still there.

Why are women like coffee?
- The best ones are rich, hot and can keep you
up all night.

A psychiatrist and his friend were sitting in a café. 'See that man over there?' said the psychiatrist. 'He claims to be able to understand women.'

'Is he a colleague of yours?' asked the friend.

'No,' said the psychiatrist. 'He's one of my patients.'

A woman walked into the kitchen to find her husband prowling around with a fly swatter.

'Killed any?' she asked.

'Yes,' he said. 'Three males and two females.'

'How the hell can you tell their sex?'

'Easy,' he said. 'Three were on a beer can and two were on the phone.'

Five Important Qualities in a Woman
• It's important to have a woman who does all the housework and has a paid job.
• It's important to have a woman who can make you laugh.
• It's important to have a woman who you can trust and doesn't lie to you.
• It's important to have a woman who is good in bed and enjoys your company.
• It's very, very important that these four women do not know each other.

One day a woman said to her husband, 'I want you to show me your feminine side.'

'Very well,' he replied, and walked out the door.

When he returned an hour later, she asked, 'Where on earth have you been?'

He said, 'I've been parking the car.'

A woman was having a run of lousy luck at the casino. Down to her last thirty dollars, she exclaimed in exasperation, 'Nothing's going my way this evening! How can I get out of the mess I'm in?'

A man standing next to her at the roulette table suggested, 'Why don't you play your age? You never know, it might bring you luck.' The man then wandered off, but moments later he heard a tremendous commotion at the roulette table. Hurrying back, he found the woman lying unconscious on the floor with the table operator kneeling over her.

'What happened?' he asked. 'Is she OK?'

The operator replied, 'I don't know. She put all her money on thirty-nine, and forty-six came up. Then she fainted…'

Good Girls v. Bad Girls
Good girls wax their floors.
Bad girls wax their bikini lines.
Good girls loosen a few buttons when it's hot.
Bad girls make it hot by loosening a few buttons.
Good girls say, 'Thanks for a wonderful dinner.'
Bad girls say, 'What's for breakfast?'
Good girls blush during bedroom scenes in movies.
Bad girls know they could do better.
Good girls paint their bedroom pink.
Bad girls paint the town red.
Good girls only own one credit card and rarely use it.
Bad girls only own one bra and rarely use it.
Good girls love Italian food.
Bad girls love Italian waiters.
Good girls wear high heels to work.
Bad girls wear high heels to bed.
Good girls never consider sleeping with the boss.
Bad girls never do either, unless he's very, very rich.

In the beginning, God created the Earth and rested. Then God created Man and rested. Then God created Woman. Since then, neither God nor Man has rested.

An English professor wrote the words 'Woman without her man is nothing' on the blackboard and asked his students to punctuate it correctly.

The men wrote: 'Woman, without her man, is nothing.'

The women wrote: 'Woman: without her, man is nothing.'

Why do men prefer blondes?
- Because they like intellectual company.

Why do female black widow spiders kill the males after mating?
- To stop the snoring before it starts.

Why do men chase women they have no intention of marrying?
- For the same reason dogs chase cars they have no intention of driving.

If Men Really Ruled the World
• Valentine's Day would be moved to 29 February so that it occurred only in leap years.
• On Father's Day, if you saw your shadow, you'd get the day off to go drinking.
• Hallmark would make 'Sorry, what was your name again?' cards.
• Instead of a beer belly, you'd bet beer biceps.
• When your girlfriend really needed to talk to you during the game, her face would appear in a little box in the corner of the screen during a break in play.
• Nodding and looking at your watch would be deemed an acceptable response to 'I love you'.
• Garbage would take itself out.
• Telephones would cut off automatically after thirty seconds of conversation.
• Any fake phone number a girl gave you would automatically forward your call to her real number.
• Tanks would be much easier to hire.
• The victors in any athletic competition would get to kill and eat the losers.

Why do men like to talk dirty?
  – So they can wash their mouth out with beer.

How is a singles bar different from a circus?
  - At the circus the clowns don't talk.

Why are men like coolers?
  - Load them with beer and you can take them anywhere.

Why are men like bank accounts?
  - Without a lot of money they don't generate much interest.

Men are like fine wine. They start out as grapes, and it's a woman's job to stamp on them and keep them in the dark until they mature into something you'd eventually like to have dinner with.

Women are like fine wine. They all start out fresh, fruity and intoxicating to the mind and then turn full-bodied with age until they go sour and vinegary and give you a headache.

The Difference Between the Sexes

• If Laura, Suzanne and Kelly go out for lunch, they will call each other Laura, Suzanne and Kelly.

• If Mike, Charlie and Bob go out, they will affectionately refer to each other as Fatty, Lanky and Peabrain.

• Mike, Charlie and Bob will each throw in twenty dollars for the bill even though it's only $32.50. None of them has anything smaller, and none will actually admit they'd like change back. When the girls get their bill, out come the pocket calculators.

• A man will pay twenty dollars for a ten-dollar item he wants. A woman will pay ten dollars for a twenty-dollar item that she doesn't want.

• A man has five items in his bathroom: a toothbrush, shaving cream, razor, a bar of soap, and a towel from the Holiday Inn. The average number of items in the typical woman's bathroom is 258. A man would not be able to identify most of these items.

• A woman has the last word in any argument. Anything a man says after that is the beginning of a new argument.

• Women love cats. Men say they do, but when women aren't looking, men kick cats.

• A woman worries about the future until she gets a husband. A man never worries about the future until he gets a wife.

• A successful man is one who makes more money than

his wife can spend. A successful woman is one who can find such a man.

• A woman marries a man expecting he will change, but he doesn't. A man marries a woman expecting that she won't change and she does.

• A woman will dress up to go shopping, water the plants, empty the garbage, answer the phone, read a book and get the mail. A man will dress up for weddings and funerals.

Why don't some men have midlife crises?
   - Because they're stuck in adolescence.

How was Colonel Sanders a typical man?
   - All he cared about were legs, breasts and thighs.

Why is sleeping with a man like a soap opera?
   - Just when it gets interesting they're finished until next time.

A man had become so fed up with going to work every day while his wife stayed at home that one day he decided to pray for a change in their respective roles. 'Dear Lord,' he began, 'for five days a week I go to work and put in eight hours of solid toil while my wife just stays at home. I want her to know what I have to go through, so please, let her body switch with mine for a day. Amen.'

God, in his infinite wisdom, granted the man's wish, and the next morning, sure enough, he awoke as a woman. He got up, cooked breakfast for his partner, woke the kids, set out their school clothes, fed them breakfast, packed their lunches, drove them to school, came home and picked up the dry cleaning, took it to the cleaner's, stopped off at the bank to withdraw some cash, went grocery shopping, drove home to put away the groceries, paid the bills, balanced the family accounts, cleaned the cat's litter tray and bathed the dog. By that time it was already one o'clock.

Then he rushed around and made the beds, did the laundry, vacuumed, dusted, swept and mopped the kitchen floor, ran to the school to pick up the kids, listened to their squabbling on the way home, organized them to do their homework and then did all the ironing.

At 5 p.m., he began peeling potatoes and washing and chopping vegetables for dinner. He then cooked and served dinner for his partner and kids. After dinner, he tidied up the kitchen, loaded the dishwasher, folded the laundry, bathed the kids, read them a story and put them to bed.

By 10.15 p.m., he was exhausted, and even though his list of daily chores had not been completed, he went to bed where he was expected to make love with a degree of enthusiasm.

The next morning, he woke up and immediately knelt by the bed and said, 'Lord, I don't know what I was thinking. I was so wrong to envy my wife for being able to stay at home all day. Please, please, let us swap back.'

The Lord, in his infinite wisdom, replied, 'My son, I feel you have learned your lesson and I will be happy to change things back to the way they were. But you'll have to wait nine months. You got pregnant last night.'

The Best Things About Being a Woman
• You can scare male bosses with mysterious gynaecological disorder excuses.
• You never have to buy your own drinks.
• You were first off the *Titanic*.
• You don't look like a frog in a blender when you're dancing.
• You don't have to reach down every so often to check that your privates are still there.

• You can get off speeding tickets just by crying.
• You don't have to fart to amuse yourself.
• No one passes out when you take off your shoes.
• You can talk to members of the opposite sex without having to picture them naked.
• Even if you're dumb, you can still be cute.

The Best Things About Being a Man
• Your ass is never a factor in a job interview.
• Your orgasms are always real.
• Car mechanics tell you the truth.
• Wedding plans take care of themselves.
• You couldn't care less if someone doesn't notice your new haircut.
• You can open all your own jars.
• Three pairs of shoes are more than enough.
• Phone conversations are over in thirty seconds.
• If another guy shows up at a party in the same outfit, you might even become lifelong friends.
• The world is your urinal.

BIRDS

The telephone rang at dawn. 'Hello, Señor George? This is Roberto, the caretaker at your country house.'

'Hi, Roberto. How are you? Is there a problem?'

'Uh, I am just calling to tell you, Señor George, that your parrot died.'

'My parrot? Dead? The one that collected three prizes at the New York bird show?'

'Yes, Señor, that's the one.'

'Damn! That's a real shame. I spent a small fortune on that bird. What did he die from?'

'From eating rotten meat, Señor George.'

'Rotten meat? Who the hell fed him rotten meat?'

'Nobody, Señor. He ate the meat of the dead horse.'

'Dead horse? What dead horse?'

'The thoroughbred, Señor George.'

'My favourite thoroughbred is dead?'

'Yes, Señor George, he died from all that work pulling the water cart.'

'What are you talking about? What water cart?'

'The one we used to put out the fire, Señor.'

'My God! What do you mean, fire? Where?'

'At your house, Señor. A candle fell and the curtains caught fire.'

'What the hell! Are you telling me that my eight-million-dollar mansion has been destroyed because of a candle?'

'Yes, I'm afraid so, Señor George.'

'But I don't understand. There's electricity at the house, so what was the candle for?'

'For the funeral, Señor George.'

'What goddamn funeral?'

'Your wife's, Señor George. She showed up unexpectedly one night and I thought she was a burglar. So I hit her with your new Tiger Woods one-iron.'

There was a lengthy silence.

'Roberto, if you broke that golf club, you're in real trouble...'

What goes cluck, cluck, boom?

– A chicken in a minefield.

A man walked into a pet store and asked to buy a canary. The shopkeeper said, 'Sorry, I'm sold out of canaries but I do have a nice parakeet.'

The customer was adamant that he wanted a canary because of its singing, until the shopkeeper informed him that a parakeet could be made to sound like a canary if its beak was carefully filed. 'But don't file too much off,' the shopkeeper warned, 'or the bird will drown when it drinks.'

Despite still harbouring some reservations about the shopkeeper's idea, the customer bought a parakeet, not least because it was much cheaper than a canary. He then headed for a hardware store to buy a file. He explained that it was to make a parakeet sing like a canary, and the hardware store owner immediately said, 'Oh, yes, this is the file you'll need. But,' he added, 'be careful you don't file too much off the beak or the poor bird will drown when it drinks.'

So the customer bought the file and went home with his parakeet.

A week later, he returned to the hardware store. 'Do

you remember me?' he asked the store owner. 'I bought a file from you to make a parakeet sing like a canary.'

'Ah yes, how is the bird?'

'It's dead,' said the customer sadly.

'Dead?' repeated the store owner. 'I bet you filed too much off the beak and the bird drowned. I did warn you.'

'I don't know what killed him,' said the customer. 'All I know is he was dead when I took him out of the vice.'

Two parrots were sitting on a perch. One said to the other, 'Can you smell fish?'

The rarest bird in the world was called, naturally enough, the Raree bird. After being hunted to virtual extinction in the nineteenth century, there was just one Raree bird left on the planet by 1905 and a huge reward was offered for its capture – dead or alive.

That last surviving Raree bird lived in Africa where it was relentlessly pursued by a hunter eager to claim the reward. After months of tracking the Raree bird across barren plains and through dense jungle, the hunter finally cornered it in a lone tree. He raised his rifle and took aim but just as he pulled the trigger a fly flew into his face, causing him to miss his target. Nevertheless the shock was enough to send the Raree bird toppling from its perch, and it fell to the ground with an injured wing.

As the hunter stood ominously above it, the wounded Raree bird begged, 'Please, Mr Hunter, don't kill me like this. Shooting me is not very sporting. Besides, that was your last bullet. What happens if you're attacked by a lion?'

The hunter thought it sensible to check whether he had any bullets left, and while he was momentarily distracted the Raree bird seized the chance to hobble behind a rock. But the hunter spotted a broken feather protruding from behind the rock and fetched a heavy wooden club from his bag.

'Please, Mr Hunter,' begged the Raree bird, 'don't kill me like this. If you club me to death, nobody will be able to identify me as a Raree bird and you won't be able to claim your reward.'

The hunter realized that the Raree bird had a valid point, so he searched around for another method of putting it to death. While his back was turned, the bird limped off, only to find its progress halted by a steep cliff with a two-hundred-foot drop.

The hunter quickly caught up with the Raree Bird and declared, 'I'm going to push you over the cliff and claim the reward. You can't fly so you'll be crushed on the rocks below. Is that a fitting way for the last Raree bird to die?'

'No, Mr Hunter, please, don't,' begged the Raree bird.

'Why, what's wrong this time?' demanded the hunter.

The bird wiped a tear from its eye and sang, 'Because it's a long way to tip a Raree…'

Two men were standing on a two-hundred-foot-high bridge with their arms outstretched. One had half a dozen budgies lined up on each arm while the other had an array of parrots lined up on his arms. At a given signal, both men leaped off the bridge and fell to the gorge below, landing with a resounding thump.

Lying in adjoining beds at the local hospital, one man said to the other, 'I don't think much of this budgie jumping.'

The other replied, 'Yeah, I'm not too keen on this parrot gliding either.'

Why do seagulls fly over the sea?
- Because if they flew over the bay they'd be bagels.

How do we know that woodpeckers are smarter than chickens?

  – Ever heard of Kentucky Fried Woodpecker?

After twenty years of marriage, a husband had turned into a couch potato who completely ignored his wife and just sat drinking beer and watching TV all day. No matter what his wife did to attract his attention, he just shrugged her off with some bored comment.

This went on for many months and she was going crazy with boredom. Then one day at a pet store, she spotted a big, ugly bird with beady eyes and a powerful beak and claws. The shopkeeper told her it was a special imported Goony bird and that it had a very peculiar trait. To demonstrate, he said, 'Goony bird! The table!'

Immediately the Goony bird flew off its perch, attacked the table and smashed it into hundreds of pieces with its powerful beak and claws. Then the shopkeeper said, 'Goony bird! The shelf!'

Hearing the command, the Goony bird turned to the shelf and demolished it in seconds.

'Wow!' said the woman. 'If this doesn't attract my husband's attention, nothing will!' So she bought the bird and took it home.

When she entered the house, the husband was, as usual, sprawled on the sofa guzzling beer and watching sport on TV.

'Honey!' she exclaimed. 'I've got a surprise for you! It's a bird with an amazing talent. It's called a Goony bird!'

The husband, in his usual bored tone, replied, 'Goony bird, my ass!'

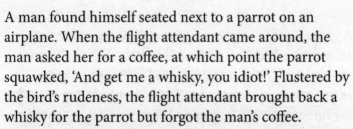

A man found himself seated next to a parrot on an airplane. When the flight attendant came around, the man asked her for a coffee, at which point the parrot squawked, 'And get me a whisky, you idiot!' Flustered by the bird's rudeness, the flight attendant brought back a whisky for the parrot but forgot the man's coffee.

When the oversight was pointed out to her, the parrot drained its glass and screeched, 'And get me another whisky, you moron.' Visibly upset, the girl brought back another whisky but again forgot the man's coffee.

Becoming increasingly impatient, the man decided to follow the parrot's lead and said to the flight attendant, 'Listen, I've asked you twice for a coffee. Now, go and get it or I'll give you a slap!'

Within seconds, both the man and the parrot had been dragged out of their seats and thrown out of the emergency exit by two burly stewards. As they plunged to the ground, the parrot turned to the man and said, 'You're a lippy guy for someone who can't fly!'

Why doesn't a rooster wear pants?
 - Because his pecker is on his head.

A game warden arrested a man for killing and eating an osprey, which is a protected species. When the man appeared in court, he told the judge that there were extenuating circumstances. 'I was simply trying to feed my hungry family,' he pleaded. 'I've never done anything like it before.'

Seeing that it was the man's first offence and that it genuinely appeared to be out of character, the judge gave him a suspended sentence.

'You mean I'm free to go?' the man asked.

'Yes, you are free to go,' said the judge. 'But before you leave, perhaps you would be kind enough to satisfy my curiosity: what does osprey taste like?'

'Well, your honour,' said the man, 'it's not as tender as tawny owl but it's better than golden eagle.'

A woman was walking to work when she saw a parrot in a cage in front of the pet store. The parrot said to her, 'Hey, lady, you're really ugly.'

The woman was understandably indignant and stormed off to her office. On the way home she saw the same parrot, who once again said to her, 'Hey, lady, you're really ugly.'

The woman was now so furious that when she got home she told her husband all about the rude parrot. He told her to calm down – after all, it was only a bird.

The next day she saw the parrot again and once more it said to her, 'Hey, lady, you're really ugly.' The woman angrily marched into the store and told the owner she would sue him and kill that damned bird.

The store owner said, 'I am so sorry, madam. I promise the parrot will not insult you again.'

That evening, the woman walked past the store after work and the parrot looked at her closely and said to her, 'Hey, lady...'

'Yes?' she said menacingly.

The parrot said, 'You know.'

A woman ran a busy pet shop in the south of France that specialized in selling exotic breeds of bird. Her supplier was always keen to interest her in unusual species and had managed to persuade her to stock bitterns, storks, cranes and herons. Then one day he turned up with a wooden crate and said, 'Edith, I've got a lovely bird for you here: it's a little egret. Look at the plumage. You stock a few of these and they'll fly off the shelves.'

'No, I don't think so,' she said. 'I still haven't sold those storks you brought in last month.'

But the supplier persisted and two days later he returned to the shop with the wooden crate. 'Edith,' he said, 'have you changed your mind about the egret? Beautiful plumage.'

'No,' said the shopkeeper. 'I am not interested.'

Two days later the supplier was back again, carrying that same wooden crate. 'Edith,' he said, 'this is your last chance, because if you won't take this delightful bird, I'll have to try elsewhere. And you know I don't want to do that. So come on, Edith. Won't you reconsider?'

'For the last time,' said Edith, suddenly bursting into song, 'no, no egrets, no, we will have no egrets...'

What kind of bird lays electric eggs?
    - A battery hen.

BIRTH

A couple were attending their first pre-natal class. So that the husband could get some idea of what it felt like to be pregnant, the instructor strapped a bag of sand to his stomach.

As he walked around proudly with his fake bulge, the husband smiled. 'Actually this doesn't feel too bad at all.'

Then the instructor deliberately dropped a pen and said to the husband, 'Now I want you to pick up that pen as if you were pregnant.'

'You want me to do it the way my wife would?' confirmed the husband.

'Exactly the same,' said the instructor.

The husband turned to his wife and said, 'Honey, pick up that pen for me.'

A doctor was having an affair with a nurse but after a few months she became pregnant. Not wanting his wife to find out, he paid for the nurse to go to Italy and have the baby there.

'How shall I convey the news of the birth to you?' she asked. 'A phone call would be too risky.'

He said, 'Just send me a postcard and write the word "spaghetti" on the back. That way I'll know you've had the baby safely and I'll send more money to take care of all the expenses.'

So the nurse flew out to Italy. Six months later, the doctor's wife called him at work to say that he had received a strange postcard from Italy. 'I don't understand what it means,' she said.

'Don't worry. I'll read it when I get home,' he said, trying to sound calm.

That evening, he arrived home, read the postcard and immediately slumped to the floor with a heart attack. As paramedics treated him, one of the team asked the wife what trauma had brought on the collapse. She said, 'It's a mystery to me. He was just reading this postcard. It says: "Spaghetti, Spaghetti, Spaghetti, Spaghetti – two with sausage and meatballs, two without."'

What is the most common pregnancy craving?
 – For men to be the ones who get pregnant.

A worried eighteen-year-old girl told her mother that she was afraid she was pregnant. When a test confirmed the fact, the mother yelled, 'Who was the swine that did this to you? I demand to know! He must answer for his actions!'

The girl made a phone call and half an hour later a Rolls-Royce pulled up outside the family house. Out stepped a mature, distinguished man, impeccably dressed from head to toe. He sat in the living room with the father, the mother and the girl and outlined his intentions. 'Your daughter has informed me that she is pregnant and that I am the father. I am sorry to have caused you all such distress, but I intend to behave honourably in this matter. Unfortunately, my personal situation dictates that I cannot marry her but I shall provide for the child.

'If a girl is born, I will bequeath her two retail stores, a townhouse, a beach villa and a one-million-dollar bank account. If a boy is born, I propose to give him two factories and a two-million-dollar bank account. If twins are born, I shall give each a factory and one million dollars. However, if by some misfortune there is a miscarriage, what do you suggest I do?'

At this point the father, who had remained silent throughout, placed a hand firmly on the man's shoulder and told him, 'Then you try again.'

A husband phoned the hospital to ask about his pregnant wife, but his call accidentally went through to the local cricket ground.

The husband asked, 'How are things?'

The reply came, 'Eight are out already, there could be another one out any minute, and the fourth one was a duck!'

BLONDES

Driving along the road, a blonde pulled alongside a truck and shouted, 'Driver, you're losing your load!'

'Go away!' yelled the truck driver.

A mile further down the road, the blonde again drew alongside the truck and yelled across to the driver, 'You're definitely losing your load!'

'Get lost!' exclaimed the truck driver impatiently.

Two miles further on, the blonde pulled alongside the truck once more and shouted, 'I'm serious, driver. You really are losing your load!'

'For the last time, go to hell!' yelled the truck driver. 'I'm gritting!'

A blonde went to the doctor and said, 'I came to see you three weeks ago, but I'm still not feeling any better.'

'OK,' said the doctor, 'and did you follow the instructions on the medicine I gave you?'

'I certainly did,' replied the blonde. 'The bottle said: "Keep tightly closed."'

How do you sink a submarine full of blondes?
   – Knock on the door.

A blonde stormed up to the front desk of a library and said, 'I have a complaint! I borrowed a book last week, and it was terrible.'

'What was wrong with it?' asked the librarian.

The blonde said, 'It had way too many characters and there was no plot whatsoever.'

'Ah,' said the librarian, 'you must be the person who took our phone book.'

How do you know if a blonde has sent you a fax?
  - There's a stamp on it.

A blonde wrecked her car. When a police officer arrived at the scene of the accident, he asked her, 'What caused you to crash?'

'Officer, it was the strangest thing,' began the blonde. 'I was driving along the road when from out of nowhere a tree popped out right in front of me. So I swerved to the right, and there was another tree. Then I swerved to the left, and there was another tree. I swerved back to the right, and there was another tree…'

'Madam,' said the officer, interrupting,' there isn't a tree on this road for twenty miles. That was your air freshener swinging back and forth.'

What do you call twenty blondes sitting in a circle?
  - A dope ring.

A blonde and a brunette went into a café and ordered two cups of tea. After a few minutes, the blonde complained, 'Why does my eye hurt every time I take a sip of tea?'

The brunette said: 'Try taking the spoon out.'

Following a bizarre accident, all eight members of a women's group found themselves hanging precariously from a rope over a high cliff. Seven of the women were blondes and one was a brunette. After hanging on to the rope for dear life for just five minutes, it became apparent that the rope was not strong enough to bear their collective weight. So they decided that to prevent the rope snapping and sending them all plunging to their deaths one of them must make the ultimate sacrifice and let go.

With time fast running out and the blondes unable to come up with a fair way of determining who should jump, the brunette volunteered. She said she would let go of the rope to save the others. She then gave a short speech in which she said she hoped she would be remembered after she had gone, and the blondes were so moved that they all started clapping…

Why did the blonde climb the glass wall?
- To see what was on the other side.

A blonde was playing Trivial Pursuit one night. On her turn, she rolled the dice and landed on Science and Nature. Her question was, 'If you are in a vacuum and someone calls your name, can you hear it?'

The blonde thought for a moment, and then asked, 'Is the vacuum on or off?'

Did you hear about the blonde coyote?
- It got stuck in a trap, chewed off three legs and was still stuck.

A blonde was trying to sell her old car, but was struggling to do so because it had 200,000 miles on the clock. One day, she mentioned her predicament to a brunette she worked with, and the brunette said she knew a mechanic who, for a small fee, could turn the counter back to 20,000 miles.

'It's not legal,' added the brunette, 'but it will make it easier to sell your car.'

'I don't care if it's legal or not,' said the blonde. 'I just want to sell that car.'

Three weeks later, the brunette asked, 'Did you go to that mechanic I told you about?'

'Yes, I did,' answered the blonde.

'And have you managed to sell your car yet?'

'Why would I want to do that?' enquired the blonde. 'It's only done 20,000 miles.'

At a ventriloquist show, the dummy said, 'We'll start with a few blonde jokes.'

A blonde in the audience stood up and said, 'I'm sick of hearing blonde jokes.'

The ventriloquist replied, 'But, madam, it's only a bit of fun.'

'You shut up!' yelled the blonde. 'I'm talking to the guy on your knee.'

Why do blondes wear ponytails?
 - To hide the air valve.

A blonde called in a repairman to fix her electric clock. He examined it and told her, 'There's nothing wrong with the clock. You simply haven't plugged it in.'

The blonde replied, 'I don't want to waste electricity, so I only plug it in when I want to know what time it is.'

A blonde at a job interview was asked, 'If you could have a conversation with someone living or dead, who would you choose?'

She replied, 'Definitely the living one.'

For their first wedding anniversary, a blonde decided to cook her husband a special meal. She told him to go and sit in the lounge and relax watching TV while she prepared dinner.

Forty-five minutes passed and he began to get hungry. He called through to the kitchen: 'Is everything OK, honey?'

'Yes,' she replied, sounding a little harassed. 'It won't be long.'

Thinking it was best not to interfere, he sat down again and resumed watching TV.

Another hour passed, and he was starting to feel light-headed. 'Any idea when dinner will be ready, honey?' he called out.

'Any minute now,' replied the blonde, still sounding frantic.

Another half-hour passed, and he could stand it no longer. He barged into the kitchen to find the room in a terrible mess and the dinner not yet even in the oven.

'What on earth's going on?' he demanded.

'Sorry, it's taken longer than I thought,' the blonde replied breathlessly. 'But I had to refill the pepper shaker.'

'How come that has taken over two hours?' he asked.

'Well,' she said, 'it's not easy stuffing the pepper through those silly little holes.'

Why did the blonde bury her driving licence?
 - Because she was told that it had expired.

A brunette bumped into her blonde friend in the street. The brunette asked, 'How did you enjoy your first trip to the theatre last night? What was the play like?'

'I only saw the first act,' replied the blonde.

'Why didn't you stay for the second act?'

The blonde replied, 'Because it said on the programme "Two years later". And I couldn't wait that long.'

A blonde, a brunette and a redhead took part in a swimming race across the English Channel to France. The redhead was first to arrive in Calais, the brunette finished second, but there was no sign of the blonde. Asked later why she didn't complete the race, the blonde explained, 'I swam halfway but then I got really tired so I swam back to England.'

Did you hear about the blonde who got a scarf for Christmas?

- She returned it because it was too tight.

A brunette, a redhead and a blonde were discussing what they thought was the greatest modern invention.

The brunette said, 'It has to be the telephone. It enables us to communicate with each other wherever we are in the world.'

The redhead said, 'I think it's the airplane. Thanks to flying, we can travel anywhere in the world in a matter of hours.'

'I disagree with you both,' said the blonde. 'For me the greatest modern invention is the Thermos flask. Think about it. If you want something hot, you put hot stuff in it; if you want something cold, you put cold stuff in it.'

'Yeah, so?' queried the other two.

'Well,' said the blonde, 'how does it know?'

CHILDREN

A young girl was attending a church service with her mother when she started feeling unwell. 'I think I need to throw up,' she said.

'Well, go outside,' whispered the mother, 'and use the bushes by the front door of the church.'

The girl went out, but returned less than a minute later.

'That was quick,' said her mother. 'Did you throw up?'

'Yes, but I didn't need to go outside,' said the girl. 'I used a box near the door that says "For the sick".'

A three-year-old boy was examining his testicles while taking a bath. 'Mum,' he asked, 'are these my brains?'

'Not yet,' she replied.

A seven-year-old girl invited a boy from her class to play at her house after school, but the girl's mother was so alarmed by their 'games' that she marched him straight home after tea. She told the boy's father that the child had been caught playing doctors and nurses with her daughter.

The father said, 'Let's not be too harsh on them – they're bound to be curious about sex at that age.'

'Curious about sex?' said the mother. 'He's taken her appendix out!'

A father and his young son went on a fishing adventure. Sitting in the boat for a couple of hours left them with plenty of time for contemplation, so the son started thinking about the world around him. He began to get curious and he asked his father some questions.

'How does this boat float?' he asked.

The father thought for a moment, then replied, 'Don't rightly know, son.'

The boy returned to his private thoughts but soon came up with another question. 'How do fish breathe underwater?' he asked.

Once more the father replied, 'Don't rightly know, son.'

A short time later the boy asked his father, 'Why is the sky blue?'

Again the father replied, 'Don't rightly know, son.'

Worried that he was beginning to annoy his father, he asked, 'Dad, you don't mind me asking you all these questions, do you?'

'Of course not, son. If you don't ask questions, you'll never learn anything.'

A little boy had a habit of sucking his thumb, so in an attempt to scare him out of it his mother told him that if he continued sucking his thumb he would grow fat.

A couple of days later, the mother invited some friends over for coffee. The boy immediately pointed at a heavily pregnant woman and announced, 'Ah ha, I know what you've been doing!'

While waiting with his mother at the doctor's, a three-year-old boy walked over to a pregnant woman and asked, 'Why is your stomach so big?'

'I'm having a baby,' she replied.

With big eyes, he asked, 'Is the baby in your stomach?'

'Yes,' she said.

'Is it a good baby?'

'Yes, it's a very good baby.'

The boy looked surprised and said, 'Then why did you eat him?'

Billy's father was crazy about gadgets, and whenever some new piece of technology came into the shops, he was always the first to buy it, regardless of whether or not it served any useful purpose. His wife had grown to tolerate his foibles, so it came as no great surprise to her when one day he arrived home with his latest must-have toy, a robot.

'Why do we need a robot?' she asked.

'Well,' he said excitedly, 'this is no ordinary robot: it's actually a lie detector. You watch. I'll try it out on Billy when he gets home.'

Billy eventually arrived home from school around 6 p.m. – nearly two hours later than usual.

'Where have you been?' demanded his mother.

'Several of us went to the library to work on a science project,' said Billy.

With that, the robot walked around the table and slapped Billy, knocking him off his chair.

His father explained, 'Billy, this robot is a lie detector. You can't pull the wool over its eyes. Now, tell us where you really were after school.'

'OK,' said Billy, his head bowed. 'We went to Jack's house and watched a movie.'

'What did you watch?' asked his mother.

'*Toy Story 3*,' said Billy cautiously.

Hearing this, the robot went over to Billy and slapped him again, sending him tumbling from his chair once more.

'Now the truth!' demanded his father.

His lip quivering, Billy got to his feet and confessed. 'I'm sorry I lied,' he said. 'We watched a DVD called *Miss Whiplash Gets Dirty*.'

'I'm ashamed of you,' said his father. 'When I was your age, I never lied to my parents.'

The robot immediately marched over to the father and delivered a whack that nearly knocked him out of his chair.

Seeing this, Billy's mother creased up with laughter and, with tears streaming down her face, she cried, 'You really asked for that! You can't be too mad with Billy. After all, he is your son!'

With that, the robot walked straight over to the mother and slapped her three times.

'Johnny,' barked the small boy's mother, 'your face is clean but how have you managed to get your hands so filthy?'

'From washing my face,' replied Johnny.

A little girl was sitting at home with her mother when she suddenly asked, 'Mommy, how old are you?'

'Sweetheart, women don't talk about their age,' she replied. 'You'll learn this as you get older.'

The girl then asked, 'Mommy, how much do you weigh?'

Her mother said, 'That's another thing women don't talk about. You'll learn this, too, as you grow up.'

Still curious, the girl then asked, 'Mommy, why did you and Daddy get a divorce?'

The mother, a little annoyed by the questions, responded, 'Sweetheart, that is a subject that hurts me very much and I really don't want to talk about it now.'

Frustrated by the lack of answers, the little girl sulked until she was dropped off at a friend's house to play. There, she told her friend about the conversation. The friend said, 'All you have to do is sneak a look at your mother's driving licence. It tells you everything, just like a report card from school.'

The next day, the little girl was sitting at the dinner table with her mother when she suddenly announced, 'Mommy, Mommy, I know how old you are. You're thirty-six years old.'

Surprised, the mother asked, 'Sweetheart, how did you discover that?'

The little girl shrugged and said, 'I just know. And I know how much you weigh. You weigh one hundred and forty pounds.'

'Where did you find that out?' demanded the mother.

The little girl said, 'I just know. And I know why you and Daddy got divorced. Because you got an "F" in sex.'

❧

A boy came home from school to find the family's pet rooster dead in the front garden, flat on its back with its legs in the air. When his father arrived home, the boy said, 'Our rooster's dead and his legs are sticking in the air. Why are his legs sticking in the air?'

Thinking quickly, his father replied, 'Son, that's so God can reach down from the clouds and lift the rooster straight up to Heaven.'

'Thanks, Dad,' said the boy.

A few days later when the father arrived home from work, the boy rushed out to meet him, shouting, 'Dad, Dad, we almost lost Mom today!'

'What do you mean?' asked his father.

'Well, Dad, I got home from school early today and went up to your bedroom and there was Mom flat on her back with her legs in the air screaming, "Jesus, I'm coming, I'm coming." If it hadn't been for Uncle Jim holding her down, we'd have lost her for sure!'

A father said to his five-year-old son, 'Did you see Father Christmas this year, son?'

'No,' replied the boy, 'it was too dark to see him. But I heard what he said when he stubbed his toe on the edge of my bed.'

A small boy was afraid of the dark. One night his mother asked him to go out to the back porch and bring her the broom, but the boy turned to her and said, 'I don't want to go out there. It's dark.'

The mother smiled reassuringly and explained, 'You don't have to be afraid of the dark. Jesus is out there. He'll look after you and protect you.'

The boy said nervously, 'Are you absolutely sure he's out there?'

'Yes, I'm sure,' said the mother. 'Jesus is everywhere and he is always ready to help whenever you need him.'

The boy thought about this for a moment, then went to the back door and opened it a little. Peering out into the darkness, he called, 'Jesus, if you're out there, will you please hand me the broom?'

A little boy greeted his grandma with a hug and said, 'I'm so happy to see you, Grandma. Now maybe Daddy will do the trick he has been promising us.'

'What trick's that?' she asked.

'Well,' said the little boy excitedly, 'I heard Daddy tell Mummy that he would climb the walls if you came to visit us again.'

A mother went into a barber's shop and asked the owner, 'When would be the best time to bring in my two-year-old son?'

The barber said, 'When he's four.'

'Mum,' said little Johnny, 'you know that lovely vase in the dining room that's been handed down from generation to generation?'

'Yes. What about it?'

'Well,' said Johnny, 'the last generation just dropped it.'

A small boy came home from the playground with a bloody nose, a black eye and torn clothing. It was obvious that he'd been in a fight and lost. While his father was patching him up, he asked his son what happened.

'Well, Dad,' said the boy, 'I challenged Toby to a duel. And I even gave him his choice of weapons.'

'OK,' said the father, 'that seems fair.'

'I know, but I never thought he'd choose his big sister!'

Little Johnny and his mother went to the doctor because the boy was suffering from an ear infection. The doctor directed his comments and questions to little Johnny in a professional manner. When he asked the boy, 'Is there anything you are allergic to?' little Johnny nodded and whispered in his ear.

Smiling, the doctor wrote out a prescription and handed it to Little Johnny's mother. She tucked it into her purse without looking at it. As the pharmacist made up the prescription, he remarked on the unusual food–drug interaction little Johnny must have. Little Johnny's mother looked puzzled until he showed her the label on the bottle. As per the doctor's instructions, it read: 'Do not take with broccoli.'

Shortly after Christmas a mother was working in the kitchen listening to her young son playing with his new toy train set in the living room. She hears the train stop and her son yell, 'All you sons of bitches who want to get off, get the hell off now because this is the last stop! All of you sons of bitches that are getting on, get your asses on the train because we're leaving.'

The mother immediately went in and told her son, 'We don't use that kind of language in this house. Go to your room for an hour. When you come out, you can play with your train set but I don't want to hear bad language again.'

An hour later, the boy came out of his room and continued playing with the train set. Soon the train stopped and the mother heard him say, 'All passengers who are disembarking the train, please remember to take all of your personal belongings with you. We thank you for travelling with us today and hope you had a pleasant journey. We hope you will travel with us again soon. For those of you who are just boarding the train, we ask that you stow all of your hand luggage in the overhead compartments, and please remember that there is a no smoking policy on this train. We hope you have a pleasant and relaxing journey with us today. For those of you who have been inconvenienced by the one-hour delay, please see the bitch in the kitchen.'

A little girl said to her friend, 'I'm never having kids. I hear they take nine months to download.'

Little Johnny came downstairs in floods of tears. 'What's the matter?' asked his mother.

Johnny said, 'Dad was hanging a picture and hit his thumb with the hammer.'

'That's not so bad,' said his mother. 'I know you're upset, but a big boy like you shouldn't cry at something like that. Why didn't you just laugh?'

'I did,' sobbed Johnny.

A little girl made a cup of tea for her mother.

'I didn't know you could make tea,' said the mother, taking a sip.

'Yes,' said the girl, 'I boiled some water, added the tea leaves like you do, and then strained it into a cup. But I couldn't find the strainer, so I used the fly swatter.'

'What!' exclaimed the mother, choking on her tea.

'Oh, don't worry. I didn't use the new fly swatter. I used the old one.'

Jenny was invited round to the home of a new school friend for the first time. While the friend fetched her mother from the kitchen, Jenny picked up an attractive vase from the living-room mantelpiece. Just then the friend reappeared, saw Jenny peering into the vase and said, 'Oh, those are my father's ashes.'

The shock made Jenny drop the vase, which shattered into pieces on the floor, scattering ash everywhere.

'I'm so sorry,' she said.

'Don't worry,' said her friend's mother. 'It was only a cheap vase.'

'But your husband's ashes…' said Jenny.

'Well,' said the mother, 'from now on he'll just have to get off his fat backside and fetch the ashtray from the kitchen.'

A preschool class went on a trip to the local fire station. The firefighter conducting the tour held up a smoke alarm and asked, 'Does anyone know what this is?'

'Yes,' said one little boy. 'It's how Mommy knows when dinner is ready.'

A small boy came home from school with a sofa slung across his back and armchairs under his arms. His father said angrily, 'How many times have I told you not to accept suites from strangers!'

The father watched enthralled through the window as his young daughter made a snowman with her friend. He heard the friend say, 'I have an idea. To finish it off, I'll go to the kitchen and find a carrot.'

The daughter suggested, 'Make it two. The second can be his nose.'

A little boy knocked on the door of his friend's house. When his friend's mother answered the door, he asked, 'Can Josh come out to play?'

'No,' said the mother. 'It's too cold.'

'Well then,' said the boy, 'can his football come out to play?'

A young boy watched intently as his mother gently rubbed cold cream on her face.

'Why are you doing that?' he asked eventually.

'To make myself beautiful,' she replied.

A few minutes later, she began removing the cream with a tissue.

'What's the matter?' asked her son. 'Giving up?'

A young girl said to her father, 'I just phoned Aunt Maisie.'

'You couldn't have,' he said. 'You don't know her number.'

'Yes, I do,' said the little girl defiantly, 'and I did call her.'

The father continued to try to make her realize that she didn't know her aunt's number, but equally the girl insisted that she had made the call. Finally, he said to her, 'OK then, if you called Aunt Maisie, what did she say?'

'She told me I had the wrong number.'

COMPUTERS AND THE INTERNET

Jesus and Satan had an ongoing argument about who was more skilled on the computer. They had been niggling away at each other for days until God became tired of all the bickering. Finally, God said, 'Enough! I am going to set up a two-hour test to determine who is better on the computer. And I will be the judge.'

So, Jesus and Satan sat at their respective keyboards and typed away. They compiled spreadsheets, they wrote reports, they downloaded, and they sent emails with multiple attachments. In fact, they did just about every possible task. Then ten minutes before the end of the test, lightning suddenly flashed across the sky, thunder rolled and the power went off. Satan glared at his blank screen and screamed every swear word known to the underworld.

Jesus simply sighed. The power eventually flickered back on, and both restarted their computers. Satan began searching frantically for his work. 'It's gone!' he screamed. 'I lost everything when the power went off!'

Meanwhile, Jesus quietly started printing out all his files from the past two hours. Seeing this, Satan was incensed.

'He must have cheated!' raged Satan. 'How did he do it?'

God smiled and said, 'Jesus saves.'

Why was the computer tired when it got home?
  – Because it had a hard drive.

Did you hear about the man whose Internet connection was so slow that his credit card expired while he was ordering online?

Why did the boy computer mouse like the girl computer mouse?
- They just seemed to click.

What goes 'choo choo choo' while online?
- Thomas the search engine.

What kind of doctor fixes broken websites?
- A URLologist.

When a man's computer printer type began to grow faint, he called a local repair shop where a friendly sales assistant informed him that the printer probably needed only to be cleaned. He added that because the store charged fifty dollars for cleaning, the customer might be better off reading the printer's manual and trying to do the job himself.

Pleasantly surprised by his honesty, the customer asked, 'Does your boss know that you discourage business?'

'Actually, it's my boss's idea,' the employee replied sheepishly. 'We find that we usually make more money on repairs if we first let people try to fix things themselves.'

'The trouble with you,' said the wife as she scratched her husband's back, 'is that you eat, sleep and breathe computers.'

'That's not true,' he said. 'Scroll down a little…'

Two young engineers, Ben and David, who were equally qualified, applied for a single position at a computer company. In order to determine which of the two to hire, they were asked to take a test consisting of ten questions. Both candidates scored nine out of ten.

After studying their answers, the department manager announced that he was awarding the job to David.

'Why?' protested Ben. 'We both got nine questions correct.'

The manager replied, 'I have based my decision not on the correct answers, but on the question you both missed.'

'And how could one incorrect answer be better than the other?' Ben demanded.

'Easy,' said the manager. 'David wrote down for question seven, "I don't know." And you wrote, "Neither do I."'

Things You Learn From Video Games
• There is no problem that cannot be overcome by violence.
• Piloting any vehicle is simple and requires no training.
• If you see food lying on the ground, eat it.
• Many nice things are hidden inside other things.
• If someone dies they disappear.
• Gang members all look the same.
• When racing vehicles, don't worry if your vehicle crashes and explodes. A new one will appear in its place.
• No matter how long you fight, you can always fight again.
• All martial arts women wear revealing clothes and have great bodies.
• Whenever big, fat, evil men are about to die, they begin flashing red or yellow.
• Bad guys move in predictable patterns.
• Smashing things doesn't hurt.
• If it moves, kill it.

A salesman was trying to sell a customer an expensive new computer which was fitted with software that would theoretically enable it to answer any question. The customer was fascinated by the idea but remained sceptical as to whether the computer would live up to its sales hype. So the salesman suggested trying it out with a test question.

For the test, the customer asked the computer where his mother was. After a few seconds the computer said his mother was on holiday in Scotland. The customer was amazed that the computer was correct.

Seizing the moment, the salesman pushed for the sale, but the customer insisted that he wanted to do one more test before writing out a cheque for such a large amount. This time he asked where his father was. After a few seconds the computer responded that his father was in New York on a business trip.

The customer frowned and told the salesman that his father had been dead for three years. The computer, hearing this, spat out some more information: No, your mother's husband has been dead for three years; your father is on a business trip in New York.

DEATH

A woman was at the undertaker's arranging her late husband's funeral.

'Do you have any special requests?' asked the undertaker.

'Well,' said his widow, 'my husband was bald and never went anywhere without his toupee but every time I put it on his head, it just slides off.'

'No problem,' said the undertaker. 'I'll sort that out for you. Come back in an hour.'

An hour later she returned and, as promised, the wig was perfectly placed on the dead man's head.

'Oh, thank you so much,' she said. 'You must let me pay you something for your trouble – and I won't take

119

no for an answer.'

The undertaker said, 'Well, if you insist, you can give me two dollars for the nails.'

After her father died, Mary was clearing out the attic of his house when she found a receipt for a pair of shoes that had been left at the repair shop in 2002. Out of curiosity, she wondered whether the shoes were still there, so she went to the shop and presented the receipt.

The man behind the counter took the receipt, looked in the back of the shop and said, 'They'll be ready Thursday.'

A ventriloquist set up a stall in a shopping mall, selling dummies and books about his art, but business was desperately slow. After six months he had hardly made any money and was afraid that he would have to close down as he could no longer afford the rent. In desperation he consulted his accountant, who suggested, 'Why don't you try something completely different? Another client of mine is making a fortune as a psychic, conducting seances. That's where the money is these days.'

So the ventriloquist changed his stall and set up business as a psychic, offering three different rates for seances – forty dollars, seventy-five dollars and one hundred dollars.

On his first day, a woman asked him about conducting a seance to contact her dead sister.

'Certainly, madam,' he said. 'As you can see there are three different prices of seance – forty dollars, seventy-five dollars and one hundred dollars.'

'What do you get for forty dollars?' she enquired.

'For forty dollars you get to talk to your dead sister.'

'And for seventy-five dollars?'

'For seventy-five dollars you get to talk to her and she talks back.'

'And what do you get for one hundred dollars?'

'For one hundred dollars, you talk to her and she talks back to you while I drink a glass of water.'

A man claimed that the secret to a long life was to sprinkle a little gunpowder on his cornflakes every morning. He lived to the ripe old age of ninety-six, and when he died he left seventeen children, twenty-five grandchildren, thirty-eight great-grandchildren and a fifteen-foot hole in the wall of the crematorium.

A chemist, a biologist and an electrical engineer were on death row waiting to go in the electric chair.

The chemist was brought forward first. 'Do you have anything you want to say?' asked the executioner, strapping him in.

'No,' replied the chemist. The executioner flicked the switch but nothing happened.

Under state law, if an execution attempt fails, the prisoner has to be released, so the chemist was released. Then the biologist was brought forward.

'Do you have anything you want to say?' asked the executioner.

'No,' said the biologist.

The executioner flicked the switch, but again nothing happened, so the biologist was released.

Then the electrical engineer was brought forward.

'Do you have anything you want to say?' asked the executioner.

'Yes,' replied the engineer. 'If you swap the red and the blue wires over, you might make this thing work.'

The priest was tending to a dying man. Whispering firmly, the priest said, 'Denounce the devil! Let him know how little you think of his evil!' The dying man said nothing.

The priest repeated his order, but still the dying man said nothing.

The priest asked, 'Why do you refuse to denounce the devil and his evil?'

The dying man said, 'Until I know where I'm heading, I don't think I ought to aggravate anybody.'

A woman married, had thirteen children, and then her husband died. Two weeks later, she remarried, had twelve more children by her second husband who then also died. A month after that, the woman died too.

At the end of her funeral, the priest said solemnly, 'At last they're finally together.'

'Excuse me,' said a relative. 'Do you mean she and her first husband are finally together or she and her second husband are finally together?'

'Neither,' said the priest. 'I mean her legs.

Did you hear about the man who was crushed to death by a piano?

- His funeral was very low key.

A new business was opening and one of the owner's friends wanted to send him flowers to mark the occasion. But when the flowers arrived at the new premises, the attached note read: 'Rest in Peace.'

The owner was angry and called the florist to complain. 'I'm really sorry about the mistake,' said the florist, 'but rather than getting angry, perhaps you should consider this: somewhere there is a funeral taking place today and they have flowers with a card saying: "Congratulations on your new location."'

A young man was walking down a deserted street late at night on his way home from a bar. It was raining steadily, so he turned up the collar of his jacket. Just then he heard a strange noise. Bump, bump, bump.

It seemed to be coming from behind, so he turned round and through the rain was able to make out the faint outline of a box following him down the street.

Bump, bump, bump.

As the box got closer, he could see that it was a coffin. Bump, bump, bump.

By now he was getting a little spooked, so he decided to walk faster, but the coffin kept gaining on him. Bump, bump, bump.

So he started jogging, only for the coffin to speed up, too. Bump, bump, bump.

He was now seriously frightened and accelerated into a sprint as he turned the corner into his street. The coffin started sprinting too. Bump, bump, bump.

Still the coffin appeared to be gaining with every step, but his house was now in sight. Would he be able to make it in time? The coffin pursued him relentlessly. Bump, bump, bump.

He raced up the drive of his house and fumbled for his keys. He could hear the coffin right behind him. Bump, bump, bump.

Sweating heavily, he finally managed to open the door and quickly slammed it shut behind him, but the coffin just burst through the glass pane. Bump, bump, bump, crash.

Fleeing for his life, he ran up the stairs. Surely the coffin wouldn't be able to climb stairs, but to his horror it could. Bump, bump, bump.

With nowhere to hide, he took refuge in the

bathroom. The coffin approached the door. Bump, bump, bump.

Desperately searching for a weapon, he reached into the medicine cabinet and threw a bar of Imperial Leather soap at the coffin. It had no effect, so he grabbed a sachet of Alberto VO5 shampoo and threw that at the coffin. Still the coffin advanced menacingly towards him. Bump, bump, bump.

In a last, defiant gesture, his hand darted back into the cabinet and this time he threw a bottle of Robitussin. And the coffin stopped.

DOCTORS AND NURSES

A man went to the doctor and said, 'Doctor, I suffer from terrible wind. It happens every time I bend over.'

'Very well,' said the doctor. 'I'd like you to bend over that chair.'

The man duly bent over and as he did so, he let out a loud farting sound, accompanied by the most awful stench. The doctor then reached for a long pole that was propped against the wall and said, 'Right, this should do the trick.'

The man looked horrified. 'What are you going to do with that?' he asked.

The doctor said, 'I'm going to open the window to let some air into this room.'

A woman went to the doctor and said, 'Doctor, I keep seeing double.'

'Very well,' said the doctor. 'Take a seat on that chair.'

'Which one?' she asked.

Patient: I've swallowed the film from my camera.
Doctor: We'll just to have to wait and see what develops.

Patient: My leg hurts. What can I do?
Doctor: Limp.

Patient: I can't stop trembling.
Doctor: I'll be with you in two shakes.

Patient: I keep thinking I'm a bell.
Doctor: If the sensation persists, give me a ring.

An old lady was slowly recovering from a serious illness. 'Doctor,' she pleaded, 'you must keep me alive for the next six months. I want to attend my favourite grandson's wedding.'

'We'll try,' replied the doctor compassionately.

Thanks to the efforts of the medical profession, the old lady was indeed able to attend her grandson's wedding, for which she was extremely grateful. Several weeks after the ceremony, she again spoke to her doctor. 'My favourite grandson's wife is expecting, so you must keep me alive for another eight months so that I can be there for the birth of my first great-grandchild.'

'We'll do our best,' replied the doctor, and, sure enough, the old lady was still around to witness the baby's birth.

The years passed and the old lady visited her doctor regularly, following his instructions to the letter. Then one morning she called him and said, 'Doctor, I'm feeling fine, but I have another favour to ask of you. Remember how you saw me through to my grandson's wedding?'

'Yes.'

'And later how you made sure I was there for the birth of my great-grandchild?'

'Yes.'

'Well, as you know I've just celebrated my ninetieth

birthday. And I just bought myself a new mattress.'

'Yes?'

'It has a twenty-year guarantee...'

A woman called on the family doctor to ask if there was anything he could do to cure her husband's persistent snoring.

'Actually,' said the doctor, 'there is one operation I can perform that will cure your husband, but it is rather expensive. It will cost $1,500 down, followed by payments of $2,000 every month for twenty-four months.'

'What is it?'

'A new sports car.'

'A new sports car? How will a new sports car help cure my husband's snoring?'

'Because he won't be able to sleep at night for worrying about how he's going to pay for it.'

Prince Charles was being shown around a Scottish hospital. At the end of his visit, he was led into a ward where there were a number of patients displaying no obvious signs of injury. He went over to talk to the man in the first bed, and the patient proclaimed:

'Fair fa' yer honest, sonsie face

Great chieftain e' the puddin' race!

Aboon them a' ye tak your place, painch tripe or thairm:

Weel are ye wordy o' a grace as lang's my arm.'

Somewhat taken aback, Prince Charles smiled politely and moved on to the next bed, where the patient immediately began:

'Some hae meat, and canna eat,

And some wad eat that want it,

But we hae meat and we can eat,

And sae the Lord be thankit.'

Prince Charles was completely lost for words and simply hurried on to the next patient, who declared earnestly:

'Wee sleekit cow'rin tim'rous beastie,

O what a panic's in thy breastie!

Thou need na start awa sae hasty, wi' bickering brattle.

I wad be laith to run and chase thee, wi' murdering prattle!'

'Yes, that's awfully good,' said Prince Charles before whispering to the hospital manager: 'I see you saved the psychiatric ward until last.'

'Oh no,' said the manager, 'this is the Serious Burns Unit.'

A doctor and his wife were having a big argument at breakfast. 'You aren't so good in bed either!' he shouted and stormed off to work.

By mid-morning, he decided he'd better make amends and phoned home. After many rings, his wife picked up the phone.

'What took you so long to answer?' he asked.

'I was in bed.'

'What were you doing in bed at this time of the morning?'

'Getting a second opinion.'

What's the difference between a physician, a surgeon, a psychiatrist and a pathologist?

– The physician knows everything and does nothing.
The surgeon knows nothing and does everything.
The psychiatrist knows nothing and does nothing.
The pathologist knows everything, but always a week too late.

A man asked his doctor if he thought he would live to be a hundred.

The doctor asked him, 'Do you smoke or drink?'

'No,' replied the man. 'I've never done either.'

'Do you gamble, drive fast cars and fool around with women?' enquired the doctor.

'No, I can't say I've done any of those things either.'

'Well then,' wondered the doctor, 'why would you want to live to be a hundred?'

A woman told the doctor, 'I'm really worried about my daughter. All day long, she lies in bed, eating yeast and car wax.'

'Don't worry,' said the doctor. 'Eventually she will rise and shine.'

A cardiac patient was told that the only heart available for transplant was that of a sheep. Knowing that he urgently needed a new heart, the patient reluctantly agreed, and the surgeon duly carried out the operation.

The next day, the surgeon asked him how he was feeling with his new sheep's heart.

The patient said, 'Not baaaad.'

The doctor held a stethoscope up to the patient's chest.

The patient asked: 'How do I stand?'

'That's what puzzles me,' said the doctor.

A man was seen running down the hospital corridor shortly before his operation.

'What's the matter?' asked the ward sister.

He gasped, 'I heard the nurse say, "It's a very simple operation. Don't worry so much. I'm sure it will be all right."'

'She was just trying to comfort you,' said the sister. 'What's so terrifying about that?'

The man said: 'She wasn't talking to me. She was talking to the surgeon.'

Doctor: How is that little boy doing, the one who swallowed ten quarters?
Nurse: No change yet.

A patient who had just undergone a complicated operation kept complaining about a bump on his head and a mysterious headache. Since the operation had been for an intestinal condition, there was no reason for him to be experiencing headaches. Eventually the nurse, concerned that the man might be suffering from post-operative shock, spoke to the doctor about it.

'Don't worry,' said the doctor. 'He's not imagining it. He really does have a bump on his head. You see, halfway through the operation we ran out of anaesthetic.'

A woman went into hospital to have her wrinkles removed, but woke up to find that the surgeon had given her breast implants.

'What the hell have you done?' she demanded. 'I came in here to have the wrinkles on my face removed, but instead you've given me these huge breasts.'

'I realize we've made a mistake,' said the surgeon, 'but

look on the bright side: at least nobody's looking at your wrinkles any more.'

Patient: I keep thinking I'm a barometer.
Doctor: Don't worry, you're just under the weather.

Patient: I keep thinking I'm a dumpling.
Doctor: Try not to get into a stew.

Patient: I keep thinking I'm an elevator.
Doctor: You may be coming down with something.

Patient: I keep thinking I'm a wheelbarrow.
Doctor: Don't let people push you around.

Patient: I keep thinking I'm a tennis racket.
Doctor: Don't worry, you're just highly strung.

A woman rushed into a doctor's surgery and said, 'My husband was asleep with his mouth open and he's swallowed a mouse! What shall I do?'

'Don't panic,' said the doctor reassuringly. 'All you

need to do is tie a lump of cheese to a piece of string and lower it into your husband's mouth. As soon as the mouse takes a bite, haul it out.'

'Thank you so much,' said the woman, relieved. 'I'll go straight round to the fishmonger and get a cod's head.'

'Why do you want a cod's head?' asked the doctor.

'Oh, I forgot to tell you,' said the woman. 'I've got to get the cat out first!'

DRUNKS

A drunk was staggering down the street turning his car keys back and forth. A police officer went over to him and said, 'Excuse me, sir. What are you doing?'

The drunk said, 'I'm looking for my car. The last time I saw it, it was on the end of these keys.'

The police officer said, 'Sir, do you know the zip on your jeans is open?'

'Damn!' groaned the drunk. 'I've lost my wife too!'

Signs That You Drink Too Much
• Mosquitoes catch a buzz after biting you.
• You lose arguments with inanimate objects.
• Your doctor finds traces of blood in your alcohol system.
• You have to hold on to the lawn to keep from falling off the Earth.
• You fall down a flight of steps but don't spill a drop of your beer.
• You only recognize your wife when you see her through the bottom of a beer glass.
• You've ever Googled to find the best way to get permanent marker off your face.
• You grow a beard because it catches the beer that's running down your chin.
• Your job is interfering with your drinking.
• You've had more than one pet named after your favourite beer.
• You focus better with one eye closed.
• All the shrubs in your garden are drunk, too, from you peeing on them.

A drunk was eyeing up a woman in a bar. He said to the bartender, 'I really fancy that woman. If I buy her a drink, will you send it over to her and say it's from me?'

'Sure,' said the bartender. 'But I ought to warn you. She's a hooker. She'll do what you want for money.'

So the drunk staggered over to the woman and said, 'Is it true that you're a hooker?'

'Yes,' she answered. 'I do it for money. I'll do anything for a hundred dollars.'

The drunk pulled a hundred dollars from his wallet, handed it to her and said, 'OK. Paint my house.'

A drunk staggered into a Catholic church, sat down in the confession box and said nothing. The bewildered priest coughed to attract his attention, but still the drunk remained silent. The priest then knocked on the wall three times in a final attempt to get the man to speak.

'It's no use knocking, mate,' said the drunk. 'There's no paper in this one either.'

A man was staggering home drunk in the early hours of the morning when he was stopped by a police officer.

'What are you doing out at this time of night?' asked the officer.

'I'm going to a lecture,' said the drunk.

'And who's going to be giving a lecture at this hour?'

'My wife.'

A large, sweaty woman walked into a bar wearing a sleeveless sundress. Raising her right arm to reveal a big, hairy armpit, she pointed at all the men sitting at the bar and yelled, 'Which one of you is gentleman enough to buy this lady a drink?'

All of the men tried to avoid her gaze until a drunk at the far end of the bar said, 'Sure, bartender, I'll buy a drink for the ballerina.'

So the bartender poured her a drink, and the woman knocked it back in one. Then she turned to the patrons and, again revealing her hairy armpit, pointed at them, yelling, 'Which one of you is gentleman enough to buy this lady another drink?'

While some men quickly finished their drinks and left in embarrassment, the same drunk at the far end of the bar said, 'Sure, bartender, I'll buy the ballerina another drink.'

The bartender poured her another drink, then went over to the drunk and said, 'It's your business if you want to keep buying her drinks, but what on earth makes you think she's a ballerina?'

'Well,' replied the drunk, 'to my mind any woman who can lift her leg up that high has got to be a ballerina!'

Driving home from a party, a drunk was stopped by a police patrol car as he weaved all over the road. He totally failed the breath test and the officers took down his details, but before they could hand him a ticket, they were distracted by a major accident on the other side of the road. Figuring that the police wouldn't be coming back to deal with him, the drunk drove home and went to bed.

The following morning he was woken by a knock on the door. It was two more police officers. 'Are you Mr Williams?' they asked.

'Yes,' he said.

'Were you pulled over on London Road last night for driving under the influence?'

'Yes, I was,' he admitted.

'And what did you do then?' they asked.

'I drove my car home and went to bed.'

'And where is your car now?'

'In the garage.'

'May we see it?' they asked.

'Certainly,' he said, and he opened the garage. Inside was a police patrol car.

A flash city broker was unwinding in a bar at the end of the working week and looking for some entertainment. Waving wads of cash, he announced, 'If anyone here can drink twenty pints of Guinness, I'll give them five hundred dollars.'

The bartender lined up the twenty pints on the bar, but nobody took up the challenge. Then without saying a word, one man climbed off his stool, walked out of the bar and returned a few minutes later declaring that he could drink all twenty. And to everyone's astonishment he did.

The broker grudgingly handed over the money and asked the man where he had popped out to.

'Well,' he slurred, 'first I had to go to the bar next door to make sure I could do it!'

A husband and wife were fast asleep one night when they were woken by a knock on the front door. The husband glanced bleary-eyed at the bedside clock and saw that it was half-past two.

'Who on earth is it at this time of night?' he groaned.

Seconds later, there was another knock, louder than before.

'OK,' yelled the husband, tumbling out of bed. 'I'm coming!'

He made his way downstairs and opened the door to find a man, obviously drunk, leaning on the porch.

'Can you give me a push?' asked the man, his voice slurred.

'No way!' said the husband. 'It's half-past two in the morning. Get lost!' And with that he slammed the door and went back to bed.

'What did he want?' asked his wife.

'A push, but I told him to get lost.'

'That wasn't very charitable,' she said. 'Remember that time when we broke down in the pouring rain on the way to pick up the kids from the school disco, and you had to knock on that man's door to get the car started up again? What would have happened that night if he had told you to get lost?'

'But this guy was drunk,' the husband protested.

'It doesn't matter,' said the wife. 'He needs our help, and it would be the Christian thing to help him.'

So with considerable reluctance the husband got out of bed again, got dressed and went back downstairs. He opened the door and, seeing no sign of the stranger, shouted out, 'Do you still want a push?'

'Yeah,' a voice replied from the darkness.

Still unable to see the stranger, the husband called

out, 'Where are you?'

'I'm over here. On the swing.'

Two drunks were sitting in a bar. One turned to the other and said, 'What's a breathalyzer?'

The second drunk said, 'It's a bag that tells you when you've drunk too much.'

'Oh,' said the first. 'I've been married to one of those for years!'

A drunk walked into a bar and started staring at the barmaid. Then suddenly he leaned over the bar and tried to kiss her. She responded by slapping him very hard across the face, and he apologized immediately.

'I'm so sorry,' he said, 'but I thought you were my wife – you look just like her.'

'You worthless, wretched, no-good drunk!' she exclaimed. 'Don't you ever lay your grubby little hands on me again!'

'Well, I'll be damned,' said the drunk. 'You even sound just like her too!'

A drunk was taking a pee in a park fountain. A police officer spotted him and yelled, 'Hey, there's a public toilet just fifty yards from here!'

The drunk said, 'What do you think I've got – a hose?'

Arriving home drunk one night, a husband cut himself when he walked into a cupboard door in the kitchen. With blood trickling down his face, he went straight upstairs to the bathroom to tend to his wounds.

The next morning his wife said, 'You came home drunk last night, didn't you?'

'No,' he replied, lying through his teeth.

'Then perhaps,' she said, 'you can explain to me why there are plasters all over the bathroom mirror?'

An elderly man was standing on his front porch barbecuing a chicken on a manual rotisserie. Just then a drunk walked past and shouted out, 'Hey, mister, the music's stopped and your monkey's on fire!'

ETHNIC

An Englishman, a Frenchman, a Spaniard and a German were watching a street performer juggling. The juggler noticed that they had a poor view, so he stood on a box and called out, 'Can you see me now?'

'Yes.'

'Oui.'

'Si.'

'Ja.'

AMERICAN

A Texan was visiting Paris for the first time. Arriving at the foot of the Eiffel Tower, he turned to his wife and said, 'They're not very clever, the French. They built this gadget over a hundred years ago and they still haven't struck oil.'

A Frenchman was sitting in an outdoor Parisian café enjoying a breakfast of coffee, croissants, bread and jam when an American tourist, voraciously chewing gum, sat down next to him.

Striking up a conversation, the American said, 'Do you French folk eat the whole bread?'

The Frenchman, who had been trying to ignore him, muttered, 'But of course.'

The American blew and popped a huge wet bubble, then replied with a smirk, 'We don't. You see, in America we only eat the inside. We collect the crusts in a container, recycle them, make croissants and sell them to you guys here in France.'

The Frenchman didn't react, so the American continued, 'Do you eat jam with your bread?'

'Of course we do,' spluttered the Frenchman. 'What is wrong with that?'

'We don't,' laughed the American mockingly. 'You

see, in America we eat fresh fruit for breakfast, then put all the peelings, seeds and leftovers in containers, recycle them, transform them into jam, and then sell the jam to you guys here in France.'

As the American peeled a messy, deflated bubble from the stubble on his chin, the Frenchman enquired, 'What do you do with your condoms once you've used them?'

'Condoms? We throw them away, of course,' replied the American.

'Well, we don't,' smiled the Frenchman. 'You see, in France we recycle them, compress them, turn them into chewing gum, and sell it to you guys in America!'

A Texan farmer went to Australia on holiday. There he met an Aussie farmer and they started talking. The Aussie showed off his big wheat field and the Texan said, 'Oh! We have wheat fields that are at least twice as large.'

Then they walked around the ranch a little and the Aussie showed off his herd of cattle. The Texan immediately said, 'We have longhorns that are at least twice as large as your cows.'

Suddenly the Texan spotted a herd of kangaroos hopping through the field and asked, 'What are those?'

The Aussie replied wryly: 'Don't you have any grasshoppers in Texas?'

A Texan bought a round of drinks for everyone in the bar and announced that his wife had just produced 'a typical Texas baby' weighing twenty pounds.

'That's mighty big,' they said.

Two weeks later, the Texan returned to the bar. The bartender recognized him and asked, 'Aren't you the father of the typical Texas baby that weighed twenty pounds at birth? How much does he weigh now?'

The proud father answered, 'Ten pounds.'

The bartender said, 'Why, what happened? He did weigh twenty pounds.'

The Texan smiled. 'We just had him circumcised!'

A Texan died and went to Heaven where St Peter met him at the Pearly Gates. 'Show me what you got, Pete,' said Tex. St Peter swung open the gates and revealed a beautiful landscape of mountains, rivers, streams, trees, flowers and all the trimmings.

'We've got that in Texas. We call it the King Ranch,' said Tex.

Then, St Peter flashed up a scene of men, women and children frolicking in the countryside, swimming, riding horses and cycling.

'We've got that too,' said Tex. 'We call it Six Flags.'

Hearing this, St Peter threw oven a trapdoor to the fires of Hell and out shot a huge ball of fire followed by a solid stream of flame sweeping over the entire area. The blinding light and heat were enormous. 'We don't have that,' admitted Tex, 'but we've got a guy in Houston who can put it out.'

CANADIAN

The True Temperature Test for Canadians

50°F above: New Yorkers turn on the heat.

Canadians plant gardens.

40° above: Californians shiver uncontrollably.

Canadians sunbathe.

35° above: Italian cars won't start.

Canadians drive with the windows down.

32° above: Distilled water freezes.

Canadian water gets thicker.

20° above: Floridians wear coats, gloves and hats.

Canadians wear a T-shirt.

15° above: Californians begin to evacuate the state.
Canadians go swimming.
0°: New York landlords finally turn up the heat.
Canadians have the last cook-out before it gets cold.
10° below: People in Miami cease to exist.
Canadians lick flagpoles.
20° below: Californians fly away to Mexico.
Canadians throw on a light jacket.
40° below: Hollywood disintegrates.
Canadians rent videos.
60° below: Mount St Helen's freezes.
Canadian Girl Guides begin selling cookies door to door.
80° below: Polar bears begin to evacuate the Arctic.
Canadian Scouts postpone 'Winter Survival' classes until it gets cold enough.
100° below: Santa Claus abandons the North Pole.
Canadians pull down their ear flaps.
173° below: Ethyl alcohol freezes.
Canadians get frustrated when they can't thaw their kegs.
297° below: Microbial life survives on dairy products.
Canadian cows complain of farmers with cold hands.
460° below: All atomic motion stops.
Canadians start saying, 'Cold enough for ya?'
500° below: Hell freezes over.
The Toronto Maple Leafs win the Stanley Cup.

Why don't Canadians have group sex?
  – Too many thank-you letters to write afterwards.

Two friends from Saskatoon, Saskatchewan, were so sick of the Canadian winter that they booked a trip to Australia. When they got off the plane in the heat of Sydney – still wearing their padded jackets, wool hats and snow boots – they wandered into the first pub they could find and sat down at a table.

Realizing instantly that there were strangers present, an Aussie local walked over to the visitors and said, 'G'day, mates. Where ya from?'

'Saskatoon, Saskatchewan,' one of the Canadians replied.

'So where are they from?' the other locals asked.

'Don't know,' replied the Aussie. 'They don't speak English.'

ENGLISH
A Geordie adored his pet dog, so when it died he decided to have it commemorated in the form of a gold statue. He went to a local jeweller's shop and asked, 'Can

ya make me a gold statue of ma dog?'

'Certainly, sir,' said the jeweller. 'Would you like it eighteen carat?'

'No, daft lad, I want it chewin' a bone.'

Two Englishmen – Michael and Robert – were begging on the streets of Glasgow. Michael collected so little money that he was forced to live rough under a railway bridge but Robert earned enough to drive a Mercedes and live in a smart apartment in the wealthiest suburb of the city.

After a while, Michael began to wonder what he was doing wrong. So he asked Robert, 'How come you make so much money from begging and I don't? I work just as long hours as you but at the end of the day your collection box is always overflowing with ten-pound notes. All I ever get is a few coins.'

'Look at your sign,' said Robert. 'What does it say? "No job, no home." No wonder you don't get any ten-pound notes.'

'So what does your sign say?' asked Michael.

'"I only need £10 to move back to England."'

IRISH

Two Irishmen were digging a ditch on a hot day.

One said, 'Why are we down in this hole digging a ditch when our boss is up there in the shade of a tree?'

'I don't know,' replied the other. 'I'll go and ask him.'

So he climbed out of the hole, went over to his boss and asked him, 'Why are we digging in the hot sun and you're standing in the shade?'

'Intelligence,' replied the boss.

'What's intelligence?' asked the digger.

The boss said, 'I'll show you. I'll put my hand on this tree and I want you to hit it with your fist as hard as you can.'

The ditch digger took a mighty swing and tried to hit the boss's hand. The boss simply took away his hand and the ditch digger hit the tree.

As the digger nursed his injured hand, the boss said, 'That's intelligence!'

The digger went back to his hole. His workmate asked, 'What did he say?'

'He said we are down here because of intelligence.'

'What's intelligence?'

The first digger put his hand on his face and said, 'Right, I'll show you. Take your shovel and hit my hand…'

An Englishman, a Scotsman and an Irishman were sent to prison. They were each allowed to bring one item with them while they were incarcerated.

The Englishman chose a pack of cards so that he could pass the time in jail by playing solitaire.

The Scotsman chose a long novel so that he could relieve the boredom by reading.

'And what have you brought?' they asked the Irishman.

'A box of tampons,' he replied.

'What can you do with those?' they asked.

The Irishman pointed to the box and said, 'Well, according to this, I can go horseback-riding, swimming, roller skating…'

Mick was standing on Paddy's shoulders trying to measure a flagpole. Seeing their predicament, a passer-by called out, 'Why don't you just take down the pole, lay it on the ground and measure it?'

'Leave it to the professionals, pal!' they shouted back. 'Anyway, we don't want to measure the length – we want to measure the height.'

Paddy and Mick were working on a wooden house. Mick was nailing down the planks. He would reach into his nail pouch, pull out a nail and either toss it over his shoulder or nail it in. Paddy was baffled by this behaviour, so he asked, 'Why do you keep throwing nails away?'

Mick explained, 'If I pull a nail out of my pouch and it's pointed towards me, I throw it away because it's defective. If it's pointed towards the house, then I nail it in.'

'Mick!' exclaimed Paddy. 'You are a total moron! The nails pointed towards you aren't defective! They're for the other side of the house!'

Paddy and Mick were ready to go home after a night out when they realized they didn't have enough money for a taxi. Just then they happened to be staggering past the bus depot, so Paddy said, 'I've just had a brainwave. Get in there and steal a bus so we can drive home. I'll stay here and keep a lookout for the police.'

Mick duly broke into the garage and Paddy waited patiently for him to reappear at the wheel of a bus. But twenty minutes later there was still no sign of Mick, so Paddy poked his head round the depot gates and saw Mick running from bus to bus and looking very worried.

'What the hell are you doing, Mick?' hissed Paddy. 'Get a move on!'

Mick replied, 'I can't find a number 6 bus anywhere, Paddy.'

Holding his hands to his head in disbelief, Paddy barked, 'You idiot, Mick. Steal a number 8 and we'll get off at the roundabout and walk the rest of the way!'

A man walked into a bar and saw an Irishman he knew sitting at the table with an empty pint glass in front of him.

'Would you like another one?' asked the man.

The Irishman looked at him quizzically and said, 'Now what would I be wanting with two empty pint glasses?'

An Irishman was sitting next to the conveyor belt at Dublin Airport crying his eyes out.

'What's the problem?' asked a fellow passenger.

'I've lost all my luggage,' he wailed.

'How did that happen?'

'The cork fell out.'

An Englishman, a Scotsman and an Irishman operated machinery at a factory. One day the Englishman caught his arm in the machine and it was sliced off.

'Quick!' shouted the Scotsman. 'Put his arm in this plastic bag and phone for an ambulance.'

The Englishman was rushed to hospital, his arm was sewn back on and three months later he was back at work with twenty thousand pounds in compensation.

The Scotsman thought to himself, 'I'll have some of that.' So he deliberately put his leg in the machine. The severed leg was put in a plastic bag, and the Scotsman was rushed to hospital where the leg was sewn back on. Three months later he was back at work with thirty thousand pounds in compensation.

The Irishman was so impressed by the two compensation payouts that he decided to stick his head in the machine. Three months later, there was no sign of him back at work.

'Whatever happened to O'Flaherty?' asked the Englishman.

'Oh, him!' said the Scotsman. 'He suffocated on the way to hospital.'

JAPANESE

On the last day of his visit to New York, a Japanese tourist hailed a taxi to take him to the airport. During the journey, a Honda car overtook the taxi and the Japanese guy shouted out excitedly, 'Honda, very fast! Made in Japan!'

A few minutes later, a Toyota overtook the taxi and the Japanese guy shouted out excitedly, 'Toyota, very fast! Made in Japan!'

Shortly afterwards, the taxi was overtaken by a Mitsubishi, prompting the Japanese guy to shout out excitedly, 'Mitsubishi, very fast! Made in Japan!'

The taxi driver had been irked by these outbursts but remained silent until they arrived at the airport. That was when the Japanese guy learned that the taxi fare was two hundred and eighty dollars.

'That's expensive,' he complained.

The taxi driver replied, 'Meter, very fast! Made in Japan!

A Japanese bride was getting married in Indonesia. On her big day, she was preparing to walk down the aisle when she glanced down and behind at her outfit and whispered something in her father's ear. Suddenly he started panicking and shouting, and all the guests ran screaming from the chapel.

Five minutes later, a jeep pulled up and three bush rangers carrying rifles and nets jumped down from the vehicle. They rushed up to the bride's father and said, 'Right, where's the giant lizard?'

The bride looked bemused. 'What giant lizard?' she asked.

Her father said, 'The one you told me about just as we were about to walk down the aisle.'

'No, Father,' said the bride, raising her eyes to the heavens. 'Your hearing is getting worse. What I said was, "Is my kimono draggin'?"'

NATIVE AMERICANS

A Native American Indian paid his first-ever visit to the big city in order to visit his distant cousin. It took the Indian a while to get accustomed to his new surroundings and to the city way of life. For instance, he had never seen a railroad train before, and while innocently standing in the middle of the tracks one day, he heard a loud whistle but had no idea what it was and so failed to move out of the way in time. Luckily, he received nothing worse than a glancing blow and escaped with a few broken bones and minor internal injuries.

After spending two weeks in hospital, he recovered at his cousin's house. While in the kitchen, he suddenly heard the kettle whistling. He immediately grabbed a baseball bat from the nearby closet and battered the kettle into an unrecognizable lump of metal.

Hearing the commotion, his cousin rushed into the kitchen, and seeing what had happened, screamed, 'Why have you ruined my perfectly good kettle?'

The Indian replied, 'You have to kill these things while they're small.'

A Native American boy asked his mother, 'Why is my sister called Full Moon?'

'Because,' explained the mother, 'we made her on a night when there was a beautiful, clear, full moon.'

'And why,' continued the boy, 'is my other sister called Harvest?'

'Because she was conceived in a field full of golden corn.

'And why is my brother called Raging Storm?'

'Because,' said the mother, 'he was created on a night of thunder and lightning. Anyway, why do you ask, Torn Rubber?'

One autumn, the Indians on a remote reservation asked their new chief if the forthcoming winter was going to be cold or mild. Since he was an Indian chief in a modern society, he had never learned the traditional Native American ways of predicting the weather by studying the sky. But as their leader he knew he had to come up with an answer, so he decided to play it safe, saying that it would be a cold winter and that the members of the village should start gathering wood in readiness for the big freeze.

However, he was also a practical man, so a week later he crept out of the village and phoned the National Weather Bureau to ask whether the coming winter would be cold. 'Yes,' answered the meteorologist, 'it looks as though this winter is going to be cold.'

So the chief went back to his people and told them to gather even more wood in order to be prepared.

A week later, he called the National Weather Bureau again and asked, 'Is it going to be a really cold winter?'

'Yes,' replied the meteorologist, 'it's going to be a very cold winter.'

So the chief returned to his people and told them to collect every scrap of wood they could find.

Two weeks later, he again consulted the National

Weather Bureau, asking, 'Are you absolutely sure this winter is going to be extremely cold?'

'Definitely,' replied the meteorologist. 'It's going to be one of the coldest winters in history.'

'How can you be so sure?' asked the chief.

'Because,' explained the meteorologist, 'the local Indian tribe has been collecting wood like crazy.'

POLISH

A Russian, an American and a Pole were talking one day.

The Russian said, 'We were the first in space!'

The American retorted, 'We were the first on the moon!'

'So what?' said the Pole. 'We're going to be first on the sun!'

The Russian and the American looked at each other in disbelief. 'You can't land on the sun,' they said. 'You'll burn up.'

'We're not stupid,' said the Pole. 'We're going at night.'

A Polish couple were delighted when their long wait to adopt a baby finally bore fruit. The adoption centre called and told them that they had a wonderful Russian baby boy, and the couple took him without hesitation

On the way home from the adoption centre, they stopped by at the local college so they each could enrol in night courses. After they filled out the forms, the registration clerk enquired, 'Whatever possessed you to study Russian?' The couple said proudly, 'We've just adopted a Russian baby, and in a year or so he'll start to talk. We just want to be able to understand him.'

RUSSIAN

A Russian man named Olav saved his roubles for twenty years to buy a new car. After choosing the model and options he wanted, he was not the least bit surprised or even concerned to learn that it would take two years for the new car to be delivered. He thanked the salesman and started to leave, but as he reached the door he paused and turned to ask, 'Do you know which week two years from now the new car will arrive?'

The salesman checked his notes and told Olav that it would be two years to the exact week. Olav thanked the salesman and was about to exit when he turned back again to ask, 'Could you possibly tell me what day of the week two years from now the car will arrive?'

The salesman, mildly annoyed, checked his notes again and said that it would be exactly two years from this week, on Wednesday. Olav thanked the salesman and once again started to leave. Halfway through the door, however, he hesitated, turned back and walked up to the salesman. 'I'm sorry to be so much trouble,' said Olav, 'but do you know if that will be two years from now on Wednesday in the morning or in the afternoon?'

Visibly irritated, the salesman flipped through his papers yet another time and said sharply that it would be in the afternoon, two years from now on Wednesday.

'That's a relief!' said Olav. 'The plumber is coming that morning.'

SCOTTISH

Visiting Scotland on business, an American stepped off the plane at Prestwick Airport and noticed a Scotsman standing beside a long table, on top of which was a number of human skulls.

'What are these?' asked the American.

'They're the genuine skulls of the most famous Scotsmen who ever lived,' came the reply.

'Like who?'

'Rabbie Burns, William Wallace, Bonnie Prince Charlie, Alexander Graham Bell, Arthur Conan Doyle, St Andrew—'

'You have the genuine skull of St Andrew?' queried the American.

'Aye, I do.'

'Hey, I'm part Scottish myself,' enthused the American, 'so my family back home in South Dakota would be thrilled if I walked in carrying the skull of St Andrew. I gotta have it. How much?'

The Scotsman thought for a moment. 'Well, laddie,' he said, 'I was told I'd be a fool to let it go for less than three thousand dollars but, seeing as ye seem so attached to it and it's a beautiful day, I'll let ye have it for $2,999.'

'It's a deal,' said the American, who produced the money in cash and left the airport happy with his purchase.

Back in South Dakota, the skull proved a real attraction at his local bar, where he arranged for it to be hung on the wall. People with Scottish ancestry from all over North America came to gaze at it in wonder.

Five years later, the American returned to Scotland on another business trip and as he got off the plane at Prestwick Airport he noticed the same Scotsman with his table of skulls.

'Hey, what have you got?' asked the American.

'I have the genuine skulls of the most famous Scotsmen who ever lived,' came the reply.

'Like who?'

'Rabbie Burns, William Wallace, Bonnie Prince Charlie, Alexander Graham Bell, Arthur Conan Doyle, St Andrew–'

'Wait a second,' interrupted the American. 'Did you say St Andrew?'

'Aye, I did.'

'Well, I was here five years ago and you sold me a skull a little bit bigger than that one there, and you told me that skull was St Andrew.'

'Aye,' said the Scotsman. 'I remember you now! You see, this is St Andrew when he was a boy.'

How many Scotsmen does it take to change a lightbulb?

- 'Och, it isnae that dark.'

A Scotsman had recently moved down to London where he was renting an apartment. One day, his mother phoned from Dundee and asked him how he was settling in.

'It's not too bad,' he said, 'but the woman next door shouts all night and the guy on the other side keeps banging his head on the wall.'

'Never you mind, son, don't let their weird ways get to you. Simply ignore them.'

'Aye, that I do. I just keep playing my bagpipes.'

FAMILY LIFE

Standing at the edge of a lake, a man saw a woman flailing about in deep water. Unable to swim, the man screamed for help, and a fisherman ran up.

'My wife is drowning and I can't swim,' the man said to the fisherman. 'Please save her. I'll give you a hundred dollars.'

The fisherman dived into the water, quickly reached the woman, put his arm around her and swam back to shore. Depositing her at the feet of the man, the fisherman said, 'OK, where's my hundred?'

The man said sheepishly, 'I'm sorry, but when I saw her going down for the third time, I thought it was my wife. But this is my mother-in-law.'

The fisherman reached into his pocket and said, 'Just my luck. How much do I owe you?'

Three men were having lunch together in the company canteen when the conversation turned to their respective sons.

The first man said, 'My son is a successful architect. He has made quite a name for himself in the industry. In fact, he earns so much money that last year he was able to give a good friend a brand-new house as a gift.'

The second man said, 'My son runs a hugely successful car dealership with a dozen showrooms in the area. His business has expanded so rapidly that in the past six months he gave his friend two brand-new cars as a gift.'

The third man boasted, 'My son is big in the city. He has made so much money on the stock market that a couple of months ago he gave a close friend a large portfolio of shares as a gift.'

Just then a fourth man joined them and they told him that they were talking about their sons. The fourth man said, 'To be honest, my son's been something of a disappointment to me. I found out a while back that he's gay. But I suppose he must be popular because his last three boyfriends have given him a brand-new house, two brand-new cars and a large portfolio of shares.'

Why are families like a box of chocolates?
  – They're mostly sweet, with a few nuts.

During a bitter row with his parents, a teenage boy yelled, 'I want excitement, adventure, money and beautiful women. I'll never find it here at home, so I'm leaving. Don't try and stop me!'

With that, he headed towards the door. His father rose and followed close behind.

'Didn't you hear what I said?' barked the boy.'I don't want you to try and stop me.'

'Who's trying to stop you?' replied his father. 'If you wait a minute, I'll come with you.'

When his young son came home from school, his father asked him, 'Did you tell your teacher that the reason you were off school yesterday was because you just had two baby sisters?'

'Yes, Daddy,' replied the boy, 'but I only told him about one.'

'Oh, why was that?'

'I'm saving the other one for next week.'

Arriving home from work, a husband was greeted by his young wife on the doorstep. She gave him a big kiss and smiled. 'You know how we've always said that this house would be better with three people in it instead of two? Well, soon there will be three of us!'

'Oh, darling!' he cried. 'That's wonderful news. I'm so happy!'

'I'm glad you feel that way,' she said, 'because Mother is moving in tomorrow.'

A husband and wife were travelling through Eastern Europe in company with the wife's aged aunt. Throughout the journey the old woman had done nothing but complain – about the food, the hotels, the weather, the people. Finally, she went too far and insulted a small nation's queen. Consequently, all three members of the family were sentenced to receive fifty lashes. However, because the nation did not wish to be seen as barbaric and backward to Western visitors, the queen agreed that each be granted a wish before receiving the punishment.

The wife said, 'I would like a pillow to be tied to my rear end.' The pillow was tied in place and the wife received her fifty lashes.

Next, it was the aunt's turn. Seeing her niece's pain, she said, 'I would like two pillows – one to be tied to my rear end and one to be tied to my back.' The pillows were tied in place and the aunt received her fifty lashes.

Finally, it was the turn of the husband. 'If possible, I would like to be granted two wishes,' he said.

The chief of police hastily contacted the queen, who gave permission for the husband to have two wishes.

'Firstly,' said the husband, 'I would like to be given one hundred lashes instead of fifty.'

'Are you sure?' said the police chief. 'That is a most unusual request.'

'I am sure. I definitely want one hundred lashes.'

'And what is your second wish?'

'I want my mother's aunt to be tied to my back.'

After winning a toy at the funfair, a father called his five children together to determine who deserved to be given it. He asked them, 'Who is the most obedient? Who never talks back to Mom? Who does everything she says?'

Five small voices answered in unison: 'OK, Dad, you get the toy.'

A Mother's Dictionary

Airplane: What Mom impersonates to get a one-year-old to eat vegetables.

Apple: Nutritious lunchtime dessert that children will swap for chocolate bars.

Bathroom: A room used by all the family, and believed by all except Mom to be self-cleaning.

Because: Mom's reason for getting kids to do things which can't be explained logically.

Bed and breakfast: Two things the kids will never make for themselves.

Couch potato: What Mom finds under the sofa cushions after the kids eat dinner.

Date: Infrequent outing with Dad where Mom gets to worry about the kids in a different location.

Drinking glass: Any carton or bottle left open in the fridge.

Ear: A place where kids store dirt.

Eat: What kids do between meals but not at them.

Feedback: The inevitable outcome when baby doesn't appreciate the strained carrots.

Garbage: A bag of refuse items, the taking out of which Mom assigns to a different family member each week, but then ends up doing herself.

Grandparents: The people who think your children are wonderful even though they're sure you're not raising them right.

Handi-wipes: Jeans, shirt-sleeves, curtains etc.

Independent: How Mom wants her kids to be so long as they do everything she says.

Maybe: No.

Oops!: An exclamation that roughly translates into 'get a sponge'.

Open: The position of children's mouths when they eat in front of guests.

Overstuffed recliner: Mom's nickname for Dad.

Puddle: A small body of water that draws other small bodies wearing dry shoes into it.

Show off: A child who is more talented than yours.

Temper tantrums: What you should keep to a minimum to avoid upsetting the kids.

Top bunk: Where you should never put a child wearing Superman pyjamas.

Weaker sex: The kind you have after the kids have worn you out.

A guy took his dog to the vet and said, 'I'm afraid I'm going to have to ask you to cut off my dog's tail.'

'But there's nothing wrong with his tail,' said the vet. 'It's perfectly healthy.'

'I know,' said the guy, 'but my mother-in-law's coming to stay tomorrow and I don't want anything to make her think she's welcome.'

A businessman in New York called his mother on Long Island. 'Hi, Mom, it's me.'

'Don't worry about not calling for a whole week. If I had a stroke, I'm sure it wouldn't be that bad.'

'I'm sorry.'

'Don't worry about not visiting me for four months and five days. If I were on the floor, I could probably drag myself over to the phone and call for help.'

'Mom, I've been really busy. I'm very sorry. But we're coming this weekend, the whole family – me, Jane and the kids.'

'Jane?'

'My wife Jane.'

'But your wife's name is Norma.'

'Is this 516-555-9416?'

'9417.'

'Oh, I'm terribly sorry, madam.'

'Does that mean you're not coming?'

A man was becoming increasingly irritated by his brother-in-law, who lived nearby and was always phoning up asking to borrow something. The man told his wife that next time the brother-in-law rang he was going to outsmart him.

Sure enough, that same morning the brother-in-law called and said, 'Are you using your power saw this morning?'

'As a matter of fact,' the man replied smugly, 'I'm going to be using it all day. Sorry!'

'OK,' said the brother-in-law. 'In that case, you won't be using your golf clubs. Mind if I borrow them?'

FARMING AND FISHING

A women's group went on a day trip to a working farm in the country. Since most of them had lived in the city all their lives and had never been near a farm, they thought it would be a new and interesting experience. As they looked around the various barns and outhouses, one woman was intrigued by an animal she spotted.

'Excuse me,' she called to the farmer, 'can you explain to us why this cow doesn't have any horns?'

The farmer considered the question for a moment, and then explained patiently, 'Well, madam, cattle can do a lot of damage with horns, so sometimes we keep them trimmed down with a hacksaw. Other times we can fix up the young cattle by putting a couple of drops of acid where their horns would grow, and that stops them. And then again, of course, there are some breeds of cattle that never grow horns. But to answer your question, the reason this cow doesn't have any horns, madam, is because it's a horse.'

With her husband languishing in jail, a farmer's wife was trying to keep the business together until his release date. However, she knew precious little about farming and so wrote to him in prison, asking, 'When is the best time to plant potatoes?'

Knowing that all his mail was being intercepted by the prison authorities, the farmer wrote back, 'Don't go near that field, honey. That's where all the loot from the bank job is buried.'

Sure enough, the very next day a dozen police officers descended on the farm and dug up the field looking for the money. After two whole days of digging, they found nothing.

Then the farmer wrote back to his wife, 'Now is when you should plant your potatoes.'

'I haven't sold one tractor all month,' a dispirited tractor salesman told a farmer.

'That's nothing compared to my problem,' the farmer replied. 'I was milking my cow yesterday in the barn when its tail whipped round and hit me in the forehead, so I grabbed some rope and tied its tail up to the rafters.

Then I went back to milk it and it kicked me in the head with its right hind leg, so I grabbed some rope and tied its right leg to one of the pillars. When I went back to try and milk it again, it kicked me in the head with its left hind leg, so I tied its left leg to another pillar. At that point my wife came walking in, and I'll tell ya... if you can convince her that I was trying to milk that cow, I'll buy a tractor off ya.'

A farmer hired a bull to service his cows, but told his neighbour that the new bull just lay around all day looking lethargic. The neighbour suggested calling in a vet to see if he could prescribe something to help the bull regain its vigour.

The following week, the neighbour asked if the vet's visit had helped. 'The transformation is incredible,' smiled the farmer. 'The bull has serviced all my cows, and then he broke through the fence and tried to service the cows in that field across the lane. He's become a sex beast!'

'Wow!' said the neighbour. 'What on earth did the vet prescribe?'

'Just some pills.'

'What kind of pills?'

'I don't know,' said the farmer, 'but they taste like peppermint.'

A farmer had a sick cat, so he phoned the vet in town to find a cure. After asking the farmer what the problem was, the vet told him to give the animal a pint of castor oil.

'A whole pint?' queried the farmer.

'That's right,' said the vet. 'That should sort him out in no time.'

The next day, the vet saw the farmer in town and asked him how the sick calf was getting along.

'You idiot!' exclaimed the farmer. 'It wasn't a calf. It was a cat!'

'Oh dear!' said the vet. 'Did you give it the whole pint of castor oil?'

'Sure did,' replied the farmer.

'What happened?' asked the vet. 'Where's the cat now?'

Pointing into the distance, the farmer said, 'Last time I

saw that cat, he was going over yonder on that hill with five other cats. Two were digging, two were covering up, and one was scouting for new territory.'

Why did the farmer plough his field with a steam roller?

– Because he wanted to grow mashed potatoes.

A man and his wife were viewing three prize bulls on a friend's farm. On the first bull's pen a sign read: 'This bull mated sixty times last year.'

The wife turned to her husband and said, 'He mated sixty times in a year. That's more than once a week. You could learn from him!'

They moved on to the second bull, and the sign on his pen read: 'This bull mated one hundred times last year.'

Again the wife nudged her husband and said, 'He mated one hundred times in a year. That's nearly twice a week. You could learn from him!'

Then they reached the third bull's pen, where a sign read: 'This bull mated three hundred and sixty-five times last year.'

'Wow!' exclaimed the wife. 'Did you read that? He mated three hundred and sixty-five times in a year. That's once a day. You could definitely learn from him!'

'Yes,' said the husband icily, 'but go and ask him if it was all with the same cow.'

While walking down a country lane, a clergyman came across a young farmer struggling to load hay back on to a cart after it had fallen off. 'You look hot, my son,' said the cleric. 'Why don't you rest a moment, and I'll give you a hand.'

'No, thanks,' said the young man. 'My father wouldn't like it.'

'Don't be silly,' said the clergyman. 'Everyone is entitled to a break. Come and have a drink of water.' Again the young man protested that his father would be upset. Losing his patience, the clergyman said, 'Your father must be a real slave driver. Tell me where I can find him and I'll give him a piece of my mind!'

'Well,' replied the young farmer, 'he's under the load of hay.'

Why did the farmer bury money in his fields?
 - Because he wanted the soil to be rich.

A man was driving along the road when he noticed a chicken running alongside his car. He was amazed to see the chicken keeping up with him, as he was doing forty miles an hour.

He accelerated up to fifty and the chicken stayed right next to him. He sped up to sixty and was left speechless when the chicken passed him. As the chicken sped off, the man noticed that the bird had three legs.

So he followed the chicken down a country lane and ended up at a farm. He got out of the car and saw that all the chickens there had three legs.

He asked the farmer, 'What's up with these chickens?'

'Well,' said the farmer, 'everybody likes chicken legs, so I decided to breed a three-legged bird. I'm going to be a millionaire.'

The man asked him how they tasted.

'I don't know,' said the farmer. 'I haven't caught one yet.'

A pig farmer received a visit from an animal welfare officer who asked him what he fed his animals. The farmer said he gave them old nuts, fruit and vegetables.

'Well,' said the officer, 'I don't think you should be feeding them wastes.' And he fined the farmer a hundred dollars.

A month later, the pig farmer received a visit from a United Nations official who also asked him what he fed his animals. The farmer said he fed them smoked salmon, prawns and rare steak, the finest food available.

'That's not right,' said the official. 'You shouldn't be feeding your pigs that well when there are people starving in the world.' And he fined the farmer a hundred dollars.

A month later, another man turned up and asked the farmer what he fed his animals. The farmer replied: 'I've recently changed my feeding policy. I now give each pig five dollars so they can buy whatever they want.'

On his way to a date with his girlfriend, a young man stopped in a field to pick a bouquet of wild flowers. He was so preoccupied with collecting the best specimens that he didn't realize a bull was in the same field.

When he did spot the bull, he also saw a farmer on the other side of the fence. He called out to the farmer, 'Hey, is that bull safe?'

'Yes, the bull's safe,' replied the farmer, 'but I'm not sure I can say the same about you!'

When their barn burned down, the farmer's wife called the insurance company and told the agent, 'We had that barn insured for fifty thousand, and I want my money.'

'Hold on a minute,' replied the agent. 'Insurance doesn't work quite like that. An independent adjuster will assess the value of what was insured, and then we'll provide you with another barn, just like the original one.'

There was a long pause, and then the wife replied, 'OK, if that's how it works, I want to cancel the life insurance policy on my husband.'

Why was the farmer hopping mad?
- Someone trod on his corn.

188

A farmer was ploughing his field when his enthusiastic but stupid teenage son offered to help.

'I don't know, son,' replied the farmer. 'Ploughing a field requires a steady hand.'

'Please, Dad,' the boy persisted. 'I really want to help.'

So the farmer reluctantly agreed and handed the boy the necessary tools for the job but when he came to check the work an hour later, he saw that the ploughed line was crooked.

'Your line is all over the place!'

'But I was watching the plough to make sure that I kept straight,' said the boy.

'That's the problem, son. Don't look at the plough. Instead, you need to watch where you're going. The secret is to focus on an object at the far end of the field and head straight for it. That way you'll cut a perfect straight line every time.'

'OK, Dad. I'll try that.'

While the farmer busied himself with other jobs, the boy set to work once more. An hour later the farmer returned and saw to his horror that the boy had cut the worst row imaginable. It went all over the field in loops and circles.

'What on earth happened?' he yelled. 'I've never seen a worse-looking field in my life. There's not one straight line!'

'But I followed your advice,' said the boy. 'I fixed my sights on that dog playing at the far end of the field.'

A farmer was upset because his faithful sheepdog had gone missing. So his wife suggested, 'Why don't you put an advert in the paper to get him back?'

'That's a good idea,' said the farmer. So he placed the ad in the local paper, but a month later there was still no sign of the dog.

The farmer's wife said, 'I really thought that advert would work. What did you write in it?'

The farmer replied, 'Here, boy.'

A funeral procession made its way slowly down the street. Half a dozen family members were acting as pallbearers. On top of the coffin was a fishing line, a net and some bait.

A passer-by remarked solemnly, 'He must have been a very keen fisherman.'

'He still is,' said another. 'In fact, he's off to the river as soon as they've buried his wife.'

A fishing club was staging its annual dinner and presentation of trophies. When the local newspaper reporter arrived to cover the event, he was surprised to see all the chairs spaced out four feet apart. He said to the club secretary, 'That's a strange way to arrange seats for a party.'

The secretary explained, 'We always do it like that so that members can do full justice to their fishing stories.'

A man phoned up a fishing advice centre. He said, 'I'm lousy at fishing and I need some tips.'

The operator said, 'Can you hold the line?'

The man said, 'No.'

Where do fish go to borrow money?
  - A loan shark.

Which sea creatures do road menders use?
  - Pneumatic krill.

What do you call a fish with no eyes?
  – A fsh.

What fish helps you hear better?
  – A herring aid.

Two prawns were swimming around in the sea – one called Kevin and the other called Christian. The prawns were constantly being harassed and threatened by sharks that patrolled the area. One day, Kevin said to Christian, 'I'm bored with being a prawn. I wish I was a shark because then I wouldn't have any worries about being eaten.'

With Kevin's mind firmly set on becoming a predator, a mysterious cod appeared and said, 'Your wish is granted'. and lo and behold, Kevin turned into a shark. Horrified, Christian immediately swam away, afraid of being eaten by his old friend.

Time passed and Kevin found himself becoming bored and lonely as a shark. All his old friends simply swam away whenever he came close to them. Kevin didn't realize that his new menacing appearance was the cause of his sad plight. While out swimming alone one day he saw the mysterious cod again and couldn't believe his luck. He begged the cod to change him back into a prawn, and after a little hesitation the cod agreed and reversed the transformation. With tears of joy in his tiny little eyes, Kevin swam back to his friends and bought them all a cocktail. Looking around the gathering at the reef, he searched for his old pal.

'Where's Christian?' he asked.

The other fish said, 'He's at home, distraught that his best friend changed sides to the enemy and became a shark.'

Eager to put things right again and sort out his friendship, Kevin set off to Christian's house. As he opened the coral gate, the memories came flooding back. He banged on the door and shouted, 'It's me, Kevin, your old friend. Come out and say hello.'

Christian replied, 'No way, you'll eat me. You're a shark, the enemy, and I'll not be tricked.'

Kevin cried back, 'No, I'm not. That was the old me. I've changed. I've found cod. I'm a prawn again, Christian.'

FOOD AND DRINK

Two lettuces were crossing the road when one was run over by a car. His friend called an ambulance and he was rushed to hospital. After several hours of surgery, the doctor emerged from the operating theatre and spoke to the injured lettuce's friend.

'I have good news and bad news,' said the doctor. 'The good news is your friend will live, the bad news is he will be a vegetable for the rest of his life.'

All the vegetables decided to take a day off from the supermarket and go on a boat trip down the river. But they couldn't decide which of them should navigate the craft along the tricky waterway.

First, a stick of celery tried to steer the boat but failed miserably, nearly running aground. 'It's not my fault,' he wailed. 'I'm only a stick of celery.'

Next, a potato took a turn at steering the boat but in spite of all his eyes, he got into a terrible tangle. 'It's not my fault,' he cried. 'I'm only a potato.'

Just then they glanced across to see another vegetable guiding his vessel effortlessly downriver. 'Who's that little fat guy in the turban?' they asked. 'How come he can steer a boat so well?'

'Ah,' replied a passing courgette, 'that's the onion bargee.'

A diplomat from a tiny Arab country was making his first foreign visit – to the US, where he was being wined and dined by the State Department. The Grand Emir was not used to all the salt in American food and was constantly sending his manservant Abdul to fetch a glass of water. Time and again, Abdul would scamper off and return with a glass of water until one time he returned empty-handed.

'Abdul, what is the meaning of this?' demanded the

Grand Emir. 'Where's my water?'

'A thousand pardons, O Illustrious One,' said Abdul. 'White man sit on well.'

Why do potatoes make good detectives?
 – Because they keep their eyes peeled.

A man went to the supermarket meat counter to buy a pack of boneless chicken breasts but was disappointed because they were all too small. So he complained to the butcher and she promised to pack up some more and to have them ready for him by the time he had finished his shopping.

He continued with the rest of his shopping until a few aisles further on, he heard her voice boom out over the public-address system: 'Will the gentleman who was looking for bigger breasts please meet me at the back of the store.'

A slice of cheese and a slice of ham were talking in a café, knowing that they would soon be made into a cheese sandwich and a ham roll respectively.

The slice of cheese was dreading the prospect. 'Any moment now I'll be the filling in a sandwich and a huge pair of teeth will sink into me. It's too awful to contemplate.'

'It doesn't worry me,' said the slice of ham. 'Nothing can touch me. I'm on a roll.'

What is the fastest cake?
  - Scone.

An old woman liked to sit in the park feeding the pigeons. She did this most days, scattering half a loaf of bread on the ground and waiting for the birds to swoop. It was one of her few remaining pleasures in life.

Then one day an arrogant middle-aged man told her that she shouldn't throw away good food on a bunch of pigeons when there are thousands of people starving in Africa.

She snapped back: 'I can't throw that far!'

Why was the celery scared?
   - It had a stalker.

One evening, an elderly English lord dined with a duchess at her stately home. The following day, a friend asked him whether he had enjoyed the evening.

'Well,' said the lord, 'if the melon had been as cold as the soup, and the soup had been as warm as the wine, and the wine had been as old as the chicken, and the chicken had been as young as the maid, and the maid had been as willing as the duchess, then, yes, I would have had a most enjoyable time.'

A young boy and his family lived in a remote corner of the country where they rarely had guests. Then one evening his father invited two work colleagues home for dinner.

The boy was keen to help his mother and proudly carried in the first piece of apple pie, giving it to his father who passed it to one of the guests. Then he came in with a second piece of apple pie and handed it to his father who in turn passed it to the other guest. Seeing this, the boy said: 'It's no use, Dad. The pieces are all the same size!'

What's purple, juicy and five thousand miles long?
   - The Grape Wall of China.

There was a big conference of all the beer producers in the world. After a hard day's work they decided to go out and have a beer together. The president of Budweiser got a Bud, the president of Foster's ordered a Foster's, the president of Miller got a Miller Lite, and the president of Beck's got a Beck's. The waitress asked the president of Guinness what he wanted and to everyone's surprise he ordered a Coke.

'Why don't you have a Guinness?' his colleagues asked.

'No, if you guys aren't drinking beer, then neither will I.'

A young bride called her mother in floods of tears. She sobbed: 'Tony doesn't appreciate what I do for him.' 'Now, now,' her mother said reassuringly, 'I am sure it was all just a misunderstanding.'

'No, it wasn't,' the young woman wailed. 'You see, I bought a frozen turkey loaf and he yelled at me about the price.'

'Well, that is being miserly,' the mother agreed. 'Those turkey rolls are only a few dollars.'

'No, mother, it wasn't the price of the turkey roll he objected to – it was the airplane ticket.'

'Airplane ticket? What did you need an airplane tick for?'

'Well, because on the back of the packet it said, "Prepare From a Frozen State", so I flew to Alaska.'

Why did the orange stop in the middle of the road?
  - Because it ran out of juice.

The Three Bears went into the breakfast room.

'I've no porridge,' said Daddy Bear, peering into his bowl. 'Who's been eating my porridge?'

Baby Bear looked into his bowl and said, 'My porridge has gone, too. Who's been eating my porridge?'

'I haven't made the damn porridge yet!' shouted Mummy Bear. 'Must we go through this every single morning?'

🐱

Why do people become bakers?
– Because they knead the dough.

🐱

Count Dracula had enjoyed his night on the town, drinking Bloody Marys in clubs and biting the necks of unsuspecting women. Shortly before sunrise, he was making his way home when he was suddenly hit on the back of the head. Looking round, he saw nothing, but on the ground was a small sausage roll.

Puzzled, Dracula continued on his way until, a few yards further along the road, he felt another blow to the back of his head. Again he turned around quickly but could see nothing except, lying on the ground, a chicken drumstick. More mystified than ever, Dracula resumed his journey, only to feel another bang to the back of his head. He turned around instantly but there was no sign of the culprit. Furious, he looked down and saw a cocktail sausage lying on the sidewalk. He stood motionless for a few seconds, peering into the darkness, but could see nothing out of the ordinary.

A few yards further along the road he felt a tap on the shoulder. With a swirl of his cape, he turned as fast as he could. Just then he felt a sharp stabbing pain in the heart. He fell to the ground clutching his chest, which had been punctured by a small cocktail stick laden with a chunk of cheese and a pickle. As he lay dying on the sidewalk, Dracula looked up and saw a young woman.

'Who are you?' he gasped.

She replied with a smile: 'I'm Buffet the Vampire Slayer.'

HEALTH AND FITNESS

John suffered from repeated headaches and eventually decided to go and seek medical advice. The doctor told him, 'The good news is that I can cure your headache; the bad news is that it will require castration. You see, you have an extremely rare condition which causes your testicles to press on your spine, and the pressure creates an excruciating headache. The only way to relieve the pressure is to remove the testicles.'

John was shocked and depressed by the diagnosis but rather than dwell on his misfortune, he decided to undergo the necessary surgery as soon as possible.

So he had the operation, and after leaving hospital realized that it was the first time in over fifteen years that he didn't have a headache. Although only too aware of what he had lost, he resolved to make a fresh start and when he saw a clothes shop, he decided to go in.

Once inside, he told the elderly tailor, 'I'd like to buy a new suit.'

The tailor eyed him up and down briefly and said, 'Let's see... size forty-four long.'

John laughed. 'That's right. How did you know?'

'Been in the business sixty years,' smiled the tailor.

John tried on the suit. It fitted perfectly.

As John admired himself in the mirror, the tailor asked, 'How about a new shirt?'

'Sure,' said John. 'Why not?'

The tailor eyed him before announcing, 'Thirty-four-inch sleeve and sixteen neck.'

'Amazing!' said John. 'You're right again. How did you know?'

'Been in the business sixty years,' smiled the tailor.

John tried on the shirt and it was a perfect fit. As he adjusted the collar in the mirror, the tailor thought he would push his luck and asked, 'How about new shoes?'

'Sure,' said John.

The tailor glanced at John's feet. 'Hmmm, 10½ E, I think.'

'That's right,' said John. 'How did you know?'

'Been in the business sixty years,' smiled the tailor.

John tried on the shoes and they fitted perfectly. As John walked comfortably around the shop, the tailor, keen to make another sale, asked, 'How about some new underwear?'

John thought for a second and said, 'Sure.'

The tailor stepped back, eyed John's waist and said, 'Let's see... size thirty-six.'

John laughed, 'Ha! I got you! I've worn size thirty-two since I was eighteen years old.'

The tailor shook his head. 'You can't wear a size thirty-two. Size thirty-two underpants would press your testicles up against the base of your spine and give you one hell of a headache.'

A woman confessed to her diet group that she had put on weight. 'I made my family's favourite cake over the weekend,' she told the group, 'and they ate half of it at dinner. The next day, I kept staring at the other half until I finally weakened and cut myself a thin slice. Well, I'm ashamed to say that once I got the taste there was no stopping me. One slice led to another and soon the whole cake was gone. I was ashamed by my lack of willpower, and I knew that my husband would be bitterly disappointed in me.'

'What did he say when he found out?' asked the group leader gently.

'Oh, he never found out,' said the woman. 'I made another cake and ate half.'

An elderly man went to see a doctor for advice on how to deal with his terrible constipation. The doctor questioned him about his diet, and the man admitted that the only vegetable he ever ate was peas.

'That's almost certainly the cause of your constipation,' said the doctor. 'All those peas you've been eating for years have clogged up your system. I'm afraid you'll have to give them up for good.'

A few years later, the old man was sitting in the lounge of a retirement home chatting to two of the female residents. 'If there's one thing I miss in life,' said one of the women, 'it's a nice piece of cheese. But I had to give it up for health reasons.'

The other woman said, 'It's the same with me and milk. I'd love a glass of milk, but the doctor has warned me not to.'

'I know how you feel,' said the old man. 'I haven't had

a pea for seven years.'

The two women immediately jumped to their feet and screamed, 'Right, anyone who can't swim, grab a table!'

A wife sent her husband and their daughter to the health food store with a carefully prepared shopping list. They returned with a bag full of organically grown tomatoes, lentils, wild rice, tofu and veggie burgers – plus, a box of cookies. The man noticed his wife's glare when she pulled out the cookies. So he said, 'Hey, this box of cookies has one-third less sugar and fat than usual!'

'How come?' asked the mother.

He replied, 'Because we ate a third of the cookies on the way home.'

Two medical students were walking through the park when they noticed an old man tottering along with his legs spread wide apart. The first student said to the second, 'I bet that old man has Feinstein syndrome. That's exactly how people with that condition walk.'

The second student begged to differ. 'No, I reckon he has Harrington's syndrome. Remember, we learned about it in class last year? That's a classic case if ever I saw one!'

Since they were unable to agree, they decided to ask the old man. 'Excuse me,' they said, 'we're medical students and we couldn't help noticing the distinctive way you walk with your legs wide apart. But we can't agree on what syndrome you have. Could you tell us what it is, please?'

The old man said, 'I'll tell you, but first, you must let me know what you think it is.'

The first student said, 'I think it's Feinstein syndrome.'

The old man said, 'You thought, but you are wrong.'

The second student said, 'I think it's Harrington's syndrome.'

The old man said, 'You thought, but you are wrong.'

'So, what do you have?' they asked.

The old man said, 'I thought it was gas… but I was wrong.'

Arriving home in eager anticipation of a leisurely evening, a husband was met at the door by his sobbing wife. Tearfully, she explained, 'It's the pharmacist! He insulted me terribly this morning on the phone.'

Immediately the husband drove into town to accost

the pharmacist and demand an apology. Before he could say more than a word or two, however, the pharmacist told him, 'Hang on a minute, listen to my side of it. This morning the alarm failed to go off, so I was late getting up. I went without breakfast and hurried out to the car, but I accidentally locked the house with both house and car keys inside. So I had to break a window to get my keys. Driving a little too fast, I got a speeding ticket, and then about three blocks from the store I had a flat tyre. When I finally got to the store there was a bunch of people waiting for me to open up.

I got the store opened and started waiting on these people, and all the time the blasted phone was ringing its head off. Then I had to break a roll of nickels against the cash register drawer to make change, and they spilled all over the floor. I got down on my hands and knees to pick up the nickels – the phone was still ringing – but when I came up I cracked my head on the open cash drawer, which made me stagger back against a showcase with a bunch of perfume bottles on it, and half of them hit the floor and broke. The phone was still ringing with no let up, and I finally got back to answer it. It was your wife – she wanted to know how to use a rectal thermometer. Well, mister, I told her!'

A doctor couldn't help noticing that one of his new patients had an extraordinarily ruddy complexion.

'It's caused by high blood pressure,' said the man. 'It comes from my family.'

'Your mother's side or your father's?' asked the doctor.

'Neither. It's from my wife's family.'

'I'm sorry, but I don't see how you can get high blood pressure from your *wife*'s family.'

'You should try spending a weekend with them!'

A man was bitten by a stray rabid dog. His neighbour called on him and found him writing furiously.

The neighbour said, 'There's no need to write a will. Rabies can be cured.'

'I'm not writing a will,' said the man. 'I'm making a list of people I'm going to bite!'

A woman in her sixties took her grown-up daughter to one side and said, 'Darling, I don't want you to think I have diabetes because I'm fat. I have diabetes because it runs in our family.'

The daughter shook her head in despair. 'No, Mum,'

she replied, 'you have diabetes because no one runs in our family.'

The Truth About Diet
• The Japanese eat very little fat and suffer fewer heart attacks than the British or Americans.
• The French eat a lot of fat and also suffer fewer heart attacks than the British or Americans.
• The Japanese drink very little red wine and suffer fewer heart attacks than the British or Americans.
• The Italians drink excessive amounts of red wine and also suffer fewer heart attacks than the British or Americans.
Conclusion: Eat and drink what you like. It's speaking English that kills you.

A cowboy rode into town on a hot, dry, dusty day. The local sheriff watched from his chair in front of the saloon as the cowboy wearily dismounted and tied his horse to the rail. The cowboy then moved round to the back of the horse, lifted its tail and kissed it where the sun don't shine.

The sheriff called out, 'Why did you just kiss your horse on its ass?'

The cowboy replied, 'I've got chapped lips.'

'And that cures them?'

'No,' said the cowboy, 'but it stops me from lickin' 'em.'

A man was terribly overweight, so his doctor put him on a diet. He said, 'I want you to eat regularly for two days, then skip a day, and repeat the procedure for two weeks. The next time I see you, you should have lost at least five pounds.'

When the man returned, the doctor was amazed to find that he had lost nearly twenty pounds. 'Well done!' he said. 'Did you follow my instructions?'

'Yes,' said the man, 'but I thought I was going to drop dead on the third day.'

'What, from hunger?'

'No, from skipping.'

HEAVEN AND HELL

Mother Teresa died and went to Heaven. She found God waiting for her at the Pearly Gates.

'Are you hungry?' asked God.

'Yes, I am quite hungry,' replied Mother Teresa.

So, God opened a pack of cheese, reached for a chunk of bread, and they began to share it. While eating this humble meal, Mother Teresa glanced down into Hell and saw the residents devouring huge steaks, chickens, lobsters and cream cakes. She was curious but said nothing.

The next day, God again invited her to join him for a meal. Once more it was bread and cheese and, just like the previous day, when Mother Teresa looked down into

Hell, she saw everyone tucking into a sumptuous feast of roast duck, turkey, venison and delicious desserts. Still she said nothing.

The following day, mealtime in Heaven arrived and another piece of cheese was placed before her. This time Mother Teresa could contain herself no longer. Meekly, she asked, 'God, I am deeply grateful to be in Heaven with you as a reward for the pious, selfless life I led. But all I get to eat here is bread and cheese, while down in Hell they eat like emperors and kings. I just don't understand it.'

God sighed. 'To be perfectly honest, Teresa,' he said, 'for just two people, it doesn't pay to cook.'

On arriving at the Pearly Gates, a cab driver was welcomed by St Peter who studied the cab driver's entry in the Big Book, then gave him a silk robe and a golden staff and told him to proceed into Heaven.

Next in line was a preacher. St Peter looked at the preacher's entry in the Big Book, then gave him a cloth robe and a wooden staff and told him to proceed into Heaven. The preacher raged, 'Why did you give that mere cab driver a silk robe and a golden staff while I, a noble preacher of the Lord, only warrant a cloth robe and a wooden staff? It's a disgrace! Surely, I rate higher than a taxi driver.'

'Well,' St Peter explained, 'here, we are interested in results. You see, when you preached, people slept. But when he drove his taxi, people prayed.'

The Pope died and went to Heaven. There he was met by St Peter and the reception committee who showed him around and told him that, as a loyal servant of God, he was eligible for any of the activities on offer. The Pope decided that he wanted to read all of the original text of the Holy Scriptures followed by every version of the Bible. This took him more than a year but the Pope applied himself diligently to the task, gradually mastering the different translations. Then one day a scream was heard coming from the library. An angel rushed in to find the Pope slumped in his chair, crying to himself and muttering, 'An "R"! The scribes left out the "R"!'

'What is the problem?' asked the angel. 'Why are you so upset?'

After collecting his wits, the Pope sighed. 'It's the letter "R". They left out the "R". The word was supposed to be "celebrate"!'

Two doctors and a hospital manager died and lined up at the Pearly Gates for admission to Heaven. St Peter asked them to identify themselves.

The first doctor stepped forward and said, 'I was a paediatric spine surgeon and helped kids overcome their deformities.'

St Peter said, 'You can enter Heaven.'

The second doctor said, 'I was a psychiatrist. I helped people rehabilitate themselves.'

St Peter also invited him to enter Heaven.

The third applicant stepped forward and said, 'I was a hospital manager. I helped people get cost-effective health care.'

St Peter told him, 'You can come in too.' As the hospital manager walked past, St Peter added, 'By the way, you can only stay three days. After that you can go to Hell.'

A priest and a rabbi arrived at the Pearly Gates. St Peter said, 'Can I help you, gentlemen?'

'I hope so,' said the priest. 'Father O'Connor and Rabbi Goldblum – we've just died and would like to be welcomed into Heaven.'

St Peter studied his clipboard for their names. 'I'm sorry,' he said. 'I'm afraid you're not on my entry list.'

'But we must be,' they chorused. 'We're pillars of our respective faiths.'

St Peter scratched his head. 'I'll tell you what I'll do: I'll send you down to Hell for the time being and if Satan is happy to transfer you up here, I'll accept you into Heaven.'

So, St Peter sent them on their way, chuckling to himself because he knew that Satan never lets anyone go to Heaven. But fifteen minutes later, the priest reappeared at the Pearly Gates.

'I don't believe it!' exclaimed St Peter. 'Satan let you come back?'

'Yes,' said the priest. 'He was in a good mood and said that for thirty bucks each we could escape from Hell and enjoy an eternal afterlife in Heaven.'

'So where is the rabbi?' enquired St Peter.

'I'm not sure,' said the priest. 'But when I left, he had got Satan down to $29.50.'

A devout nun died and ascended to Heaven. On arrival, she was told by St Peter that she could meet whoever she wanted while her room was being prepared. She replied gently that if it were possible she would like an audience with the Virgin Mary. St Peter instantly agreed to the request and escorted the nun to a little door in an outbuilding.

He knocked softly on the door and a murmured reply came from within, bidding them to enter. As the door was opened, the nun saw a middle-aged Jewish woman in the garb of the first century, quietly knitting.

The nun sat reverently for some time at Mary's feet and finally gestured as if to ask a question. Mary looked up from her knitting and indicated that it was permissible to ask.

'Holy Mother, please tell me,' began the nun, 'you were chosen from all women to be the mother of God. You are a simple woman, I know. But could you just give me an inkling of what it felt like when it happened, when Jesus was born?'

With a distant look in her eyes, Mary replied, 'Well, really, I wanted a girl.'

LAW AND ORDER

A ruthless bank robber walked over to one of his hostages and snarled, 'Did you see my face?'

'Yes, I did,' said the hostage boldly.

And the robber shot him dead.

Then, he turned to the next man and asked, 'Did you see my face?'

'No,' replied the man. "But I think my wife may have done.'

Tried for murder in a hostile town, a man thought he had no chance of getting off, so just before the jury

219

retired he bribed one of the jurors to find him guilty of the lesser crime of manslaughter.

The jury were out for four days before they eventually returned a verdict of manslaughter. The relieved defendant sought out the bribed juror and said, 'Thank you. How did you manage to swing it?'

'It wasn't easy,' admitted the juror. 'All the others wanted to acquit you.'

Police are on the lookout for a cross-eyed burglar. They have told the public: 'If you see him peering in your front window, please warn the people next door.'

Did you hear about the thief who stole from a blood bank?
   – He was caught red-handed.

A man was driving through a crime-ridden, run-down part of town when his car broke down. While he was looking under the bonnet to see what the problem was, he heard a thud and saw someone taking things out of the boot.

'Hey! This is my car!' yelled the driver.

'OK,' said the thief. 'You take the front and I'll take the back.'

Three rookie cops were training to become detectives. To test their skills in recognizing a suspect, the chief of detectives showed each trainee a picture for five seconds and then hid it.

Showing the picture to the first rookie, he said, 'This is your suspect. How would you recognize him?'

'That's easy,' said the first rookie. 'We'd catch him straight away because he's only got one eye.'

'Uh, that's because the picture shows his profile,' explained the chief.

Dismayed by the first rookie's response, the chief turned to the second trainee. Showing him the same picture for five seconds, the chief said, 'This is your suspect. How would you recognize him?'

'No problem,' said the second rookie confidently. 'He'd be easy to catch because he's only got one ear.'

The chief was almost lost for words. 'What's wrong with you two idiots?' he raged. 'Of course only one eye and one ear are showing – that's because it's a picture of his profile! Is that the best answer you can come up with?'

Despairing of the quality of the candidates, the chief turned to the third rookie, showed him the same picture and said gruffly, 'This is your suspect. How would you recognize him? And don't you dare give me another stupid answer.'

The third rookie studied the picture intently and then declared, 'The suspect wears contact lenses.'

The chief was impressed by the answer and said, 'Wait while I check his file to see if he does wear contact lenses.' The chief then checked on the computer. 'Hey, how about that!' he beamed. 'It's true. The suspect does wear contact lenses. That's a brilliant piece of deduction. How did you work it out just from looking at the picture?'

The third rookie replied, 'It was easy. He can't wear regular glasses because he only has one eye and one ear.'

The police chief asked a new recruit, 'Have you ever seen a lie detector?'

  - 'Better than that, chief. I married one!'

A cross-eyed judge looked at the three defendants in the dock and said to the first one, 'How do you plead?'

'Not guilty,' said the second defendant.

'I wasn't talking to you,' roared the judge.

'I never said a word,' replied the third defendant.

Things Not to Say to a Police Officer

- I can't reach my driving licence unless you hold my beer.
- Oh, sorry, that's the fake licence. Here's the real one.
- You're not gonna check the boot, are you?
- No, I don't know how fast I was going. The little needle stops at 110mph.
- Aren't you the guy from the Village People?
- Sorry, officer, I didn't realize my radar detector wasn't plugged in.
- If you took some of the stuff I've just had, you wouldn't be so uptight.
- Is it true that people become cops because they're too dumb to work at McDonald's?
- Thanks, officer. The last cop let me off with a warning, too.

Three men were sitting at a bar complaining about the injustices of the legal system.

One said, 'A friend of mine ended up in court for dropping a cigarette packet.'

The other two shook their heads knowingly.

The second said, 'A friend of mine has got a criminal record because he overfilled his garbage bin.'

The other two shook their heads sadly.

The third said, 'That's nothing. A friend of mine was prosecuted on account of his beliefs. He believed he could drive after eight pints!'

Did you hear about the identical twins who robbed a bank?
   - After they were caught, they finished each other's sentences.

Three prisoners were about to face a firing squad. Before their execution, they were given the choice of what they would like to eat for their last meal.

The first prisoner asked for a juicy steak. He was served the steak and then taken away to be shot.

The second prisoner requested roast duck. He was served the duck and then taken away to be shot.

The third prisoner asked for strawberries.

'Strawberries?' queried the guards. 'But they're not in season.'

'It's OK,' said the prisoner. 'I'll wait!'

Two assassins had been hired to kill a leading politician as he arrived for work. They monitored the politician's daily movements for three months and observed that he was extremely punctual, always arriving at his office at 9 a.m. precisely. So on the day of the hit they made their way to the roof of a building opposite his office at 8.45 a.m. and waited for him to show.

But by 9.15, there was still no sign of him. The would-be assassins were growing anxious.

'I can't understand it,' said one. 'He's never been as much as a minute late before.'

'Yes, it's very odd,' agreed the other. 'I hope nothing's happened to him.'

A traffic cop stopped a motorist and asked, 'Is this car licensed?'

'Of course it is,' said the driver.

'Great,' said the cop. 'I'll have a pint.'

A police officer stopped a suspicious-looking man in the street and asked, 'Where were you between four and six?'

The man replied, 'Primary school.'

Arriving home to find that her house had been robbed, a woman called the police and insisted they send a patrol car over straight away.

'I'm afraid the only car we have in your area at the moment,' said the dispatcher, 'is a canine car.'

'I don't care,' shouted the woman. 'Just send him over!'

A few minutes later the police car pulled up, but when the woman saw the officer get out with his German shepherd, she wailed, 'Just my luck! My house gets robbed and they send me a blind policeman!'

Why did the policeman put handcuffs on the building?
   - He was making a house arrest.

Before a high-profile criminal trial could get underway, the jury selection process lasted for several days with both sides objecting to prospective jurors on the grounds that their views had already been prejudiced by sensational newspaper articles about the case.

One man was called forward to be questioned.

'Are you a property owner?' asked the judge.

'I am, your honour.'

'Married or single?'

'Married for thirty-five years, your honour.'

'Formed or expressed an opinion?'

The man replied, 'Not in thirty-five years, your honour.'

The judge said to the defendant, 'What is your occupation?'

'I'm a locksmith, your honour.'

'Well, would you explain to me what a locksmith was doing in a jeweller's shop at half-past two in the morning?'

The defendant replied: 'I was making a bolt for the door.'

Why was the sword swallower sent to prison?
  – He coughed, and killed two people.

The judge frowned at the defendant and said, 'So you admit to breaking into Johnson's department store in the High Street on three occasions?'

'Yes, your honour.'

'And why did you break in?'

'Because my wife wanted a dress.'

The judge checked his records. 'But it says here that you broke in three nights in a row.'

'That's right, your honour. She made me exchange it twice.'

A woman was walking along the street one evening when a stranger ran up to her and said, 'Have you seen a policeman?'

'No, I haven't,' she replied.

'Good,' said the stranger. 'Hand over your purse.'

A gunman burst into a bank and yelled at the cashier, 'Hand over the money or you're geography!'

The cashier said, 'Don't you mean history?'

The robber shouted, 'Don't change the subject.'

The sheriff of a small town was also the local vet. One night the phone rang and his wife answered.

An agitated voice enquired, 'Is your husband there?'

'Yes,' said the wife. 'Do you require his services as sheriff or vet?'

'Both,' said the caller. 'We can't get our dog's mouth open, and there's a burglar in it.'

A police officer pulled over a man for erratic driving and asked him to step out of the car. After looking at the man closely, he said, 'I can't help noticing, sir, that your eyes are bloodshot. Have you been drinking?'

The man replied indignantly, 'Officer, I can't help noticing your eyes are glazed. Have you been eating doughnuts?'

How did the police find a suspect standing on a set of bathroom scales?
 – He gave himself a weigh.

A shoplifter was caught red-handed trying to steal a necklace from an exclusive jewellery store.

He decided to plead with the store manager. 'I know you don't need all the trouble of notifying the police and going to court, so why don't we settle this amicably? If I agree to buy the necklace, we can forget about the whole thing.'

The manager thought about it for a minute, then said, 'OK', and wrote out the sales slip.

The thief looked at the slip and said, 'This is a bit more than I intended to spend. Can you show me something less expensive?'

A young woman was appearing in court as a character witness at the trial of a friend. Attempting to discredit her testimony, the prosecution barrister asked her, 'Is it true that on August 5 last year you performed an act of gross indecency with a one-legged dwarf, who was waving a Union Jack at the time, on the roof of a car while speeding at 80mph through the centre of London?'

The woman replied, 'What was the date again?'

A farmer was pulled over by a police officer for a minor speeding violation. The officer proceeded to deliver a patronizing lecture about safe driving, making the farmer feel like a small boy. The farmer was distinctly unimpressed by the officer's high-handed manner. When he finally got round to writing the ticket, the officer was troubled by some flies that were circling around his head.

'Ya having problems with circle flies, are ya?' enquired the farmer.

'Whatever they are, these flies are certainly a damned nuisance,' replied the officer. 'I can't say I've ever heard of circle flies.'

'Circle flies are common on farms,' continued the farmer. 'Ya see, they call 'em circle flies 'cause they're almost always found circling the back end of a horse.'

'Oh, right,' said the officer, but then he suddenly stopped writing the ticket. 'Wait a minute, are you trying to call me a horse's ass?'

'No, officer,' the farmer answered defensively. 'I have far too much respect for the police to call you a horse's ass.'

'That's OK then,' said the officer, resuming writing the ticket.

After a short pause the farmer added, 'Hard to fool them flies though.'

What were the gangster's last words?
- 'Who put that violin in my violin case?'

A young prisoner found himself sharing a cell with an older man who had spent much of his life behind bars. One day they started discussing their respective pasts. 'Look at me,' said the older man. 'I'm old and worn out now, but believe it or not I used to live the life of Riley. I stayed in the smartest hotels on the French Riviera, ate in the finest restaurants. I had a yacht, fast cars and beautiful women.'

'What happened?' asked his young cellmate.

'One day, Riley reported his credit cards missing.'

A man had to take a day off work to appear in court on a minor charge. After waiting all day for his case to be heard, he was finally called before the judge late in the afternoon. But no sooner had the defendant stood in the dock than the judge announced that the court would be adjourned until the following day.

'This is crazy!' shouted the defendant angrily.

Tired at the end of a long day, the judge rapped back, 'I fine you twenty dollars for contempt of court!'

Then, noticing the defendant checking his wallet, the judge softened and said, 'It's all right. You don't have to pay right now.'

'I wasn't going to,' replied the defendant. 'I was just seeing if I'd got enough money for two more words!

Did you hear about the men who were arrested for throwing bombs from a boat?

- They dropped the charges.

It was Christmas Day but all police leave in town was cancelled following a shooting in the park. Officers searched the area for evidence relating to the gun but could find nothing until one keen young detective took a closer look at the only deciduous tree in the park – a huge oak that, because it was winter, had lost all its leaves. Sure enough, within a couple of minutes he had found the spent bullet casing from the shooting.

'How did you know where to look?' asked his senior officer.

'It was obvious when you think about it,' replied the young detective. 'What do you associate with the first day of Christmas? A cartridge in a bare tree.'

LAWYERS

A lawyer was trying to give his teenage son some career advice. 'Why on earth do you want to be a doctor instead of a lawyer?' he asked. 'The law is a noble profession. What's wrong with lawyers?'

'Well, Dad,' explained the boy, 'I really want to help people. And when was the last time you heard someone stand up in a crowd and shout frantically, "Is there a lawyer in the house?"'

A judge was hearing a drink-driving case but the defendant, who had a long criminal record, demanded trial by jury. It was nearly four o'clock in the afternoon and because forming a jury would take some time, the judge called a recess and went out in the hall to recruit anyone available for jury duty. In the main lobby, he found a dozen lawyers and told them that they were to be the jury. The lawyers thought this would be a new experience and followed the judge back into the courtroom.

The prosecution and defence cases were heard in little over twenty minutes, and it was obvious that the defendant was guilty. The jurors retired to their room, and the judge, thinking that they would return with their verdict in a matter of minutes, prepared to go home. But after three days and nights, the jury of lawyers was still out. The judge was furious and eventually sent the bailiff into the jury room to find out what was delaying the verdict.

When the bailiff returned, the judge said impatiently, 'Well, have they reached a verdict yet?'

The bailiff shook his head and said, 'Verdict? They're still arguing over who should be foreman!'

Judge: Have you anything to offer to this court before I pass sentence?

Defendant: No, your honour. My lawyer took every penny.

A butcher was standing behind the counter of his shop one day when a dog ran in, grabbed some sausages off the counter and ran out with them in his mouth. The butcher recognized the dog as belonging to the lawyer in the office next door, so he went round and said, 'Your dog just stole some sausages from my shop. I believe you owe me for the meat.'

'That is correct,' replied the lawyer. 'What was the value of the sausages?'

'$3.50,' said the butcher.

'Very well,' said the lawyer. 'You will receive a cheque for that amount in the mail tomorrow.'

The next day, the butcher received a cheque for $3.50… along with a bill for $150 in respect of 'legal consultation'.

Norman needed a lawyer, so he looked through the Yellow Pages and picked out a law firm – Schwartz, Schwartz, Schwartz & Schwartz.He called up and said, 'Is Mr. Schwartz in?'The man said, 'No, he's out playing golf.'Norman said, 'All right, then let me speak to Mr Schwartz.'He's not with the firm any more; he's retired.''Then let me talk to Mr Schwartz.''He's away in Chicago – he won't be back for a month.''OK, then let me talk to the other Mr Schwartz.''Speaking!'

A middle-aged, balding man walked into a post office and stood at the counter spraying perfume over bright-pink envelopes and then sticking special Valentine's Day stamps on them.

The man behind him in the queue asked impatiently, 'What are you doing?'

'I'm sending out three hundred Valentine's cards signed "Guess who?"'

'Why?'

'I'm a divorce lawyer.'

What's the definition of a lawyer?

– The larval stage of a politician.

A man was acquitted of stealing a Ferrari, but after the case he returned to court and told the trial judge, 'I want to get a warrant out for that no-good lawyer of mine.'

'But your lawyer got you acquitted,' said the judge, puzzled. 'Why do you want him arrested?'

'Well, your honour,' said the man, 'I didn't have the money to pay his fee, so he went and took the car I stole.'

An airplane was experiencing engine trouble so the pilot instructed the cabin crew to have the passengers take their seats and prepare for an emergency landing. A few minutes later, the pilot asked the flight attendants if everyone was buckled in and ready. 'All set back here, captain,' came the reply, 'except one lawyer who is still going around handing out business cards.'

What do you call a lawyer who doesn't chase ambulances?

– Retired.

The judge called the opposing lawyers in a high-profile criminal trial into his chambers to discuss their conduct. 'Right,' he began, 'both of you have attempted to pervert the course of justice by offering me a bribe. You, Mr Kennedy, gave me $15,000, and you, Mr Jeffries, gave me $10,000.'

As the lawyers squirmed uncomfortably, the judge reached into his pocket and pulled out a cheque. Handing it to Kennedy, the judge said, 'I am returning $5,000 to you, and we're going to try this case solely on its merits.'

A car mechanic noticed that the car which had just been brought in for repair was covered with leaves, grass, branches, dirt and blood. He asked the driver, 'What happened here?'

The driver explained, 'I ran into a lawyer.'

'Right,' said the mechanic, 'that explains the blood.

But what about the leaves, the grass, the branches and the dirt?'

'I had to chase him through the park.'

Why are lawyers banned from having sex with their clients?
- To stop the client being billed twice for the same service.

Three surgeons met at a convention and during a break in proceedings they discussed what type of patients they preferred to operate on.

The first said, 'I like to operate on short people because it's more of a challenge to get the job done without making a large incision.'

The second said, 'I like to operate on Oriental people because their anatomy is always textbook perfect.'

The third said, 'I like to operate on lawyers because they are by far the easiest. When you open them up, you'll see that they have no heart, certainly no guts, and their rear end is interchangeable with their mouth.'

A man went to his lawyer and said, 'I want to make a will but I'm not sure how to go about it.'

The lawyer replied, 'Just leave it all to me.'

The man looked horrified. 'Well, I knew you'd be taking a large slice, but I was hoping to leave some to my children!'

What's the difference between a lawyer and a leech?
 – A leech will let go when its victim dies.

A prominent middle-aged attorney was walking in the woods when he heard a booming voice from above say, 'You are going to live to be a hundred.' That must be God speaking, the attorney thought.

Immediately he began doing good deeds, figuring that he now had ample time to make amends in order to enter Heaven. But as he left the homeless shelter where he had just volunteered an hour of his services, he was hit by a bus and killed.

Coming face to face with God, the attorney protested, 'You promised me I was going to live to be a hundred. Instead, the very first day I did a good deed, I got hit by a bus and here I am. Why?'

'I didn't recognize you,' replied God.

Defending a wealthy businessman in a complex lawsuit, a young lawyer felt the case was going against him. In desperation he asked the senior partner at the law firm whether it might be worth sending the judge a box of his favourite cigars.

'Do that and you'll be sure to lose!' said the senior partner, horrified. 'The judge is an honourable man and would not take kindly to a bribe.'

Eventually, the judge ruled in favour of the businessman, and the senior partner took the young lawyer out to lunch to congratulate him. 'Aren't you glad?' he said, 'that you didn't send those cigars to the judge?'

'I did send them,' said the lawyer. 'But I enclosed the business card of the plaintiff's lawyer!'

MARRIAGE AND DIVORCE

A husband arrived home late one night from a poker evening with his friends. His wife was waiting to lay down the law.

'Stop!' he said. 'Don't even bother having a go at me. Pack your bags! I lost you in the poker game, so you're moving in with Brian.'

'How could you do such a terrible thing?' she cried.

'It wasn't easy,' he said. 'You don't normally fold with four aces.'

Early in their marriage, a young bride turned to her husband and said, 'I know it can be difficult for men to read women's moods, so here are a few pointers: in the evening, if my hair is neat and tidy, that means I don't want sex at all; if my hair is a little dishevelled, that means I may or may not want sex; and if my hair is wild and untamed, that means I want sex.'

'OK, sweetheart,' replied the groom. 'Just remember that when I come home from work, I usually like a drink. If I have only one drink, that means I don't want sex; if I have two drinks, I may or may not want sex; and if I have three drinks, the state of your hair becomes irrelevant.'

A woman passenger on a bus tapped a man on the leg and said, 'You're not married, are you?'

'No, I'm not,' he answered. 'How can you tell?'

'Because,' she said, 'when you offered me your seat, you left it up.'

A girl came home from a date looking rather sad. 'What's the matter?' asked her mother.

'Nigel has asked me to marry him,' said the girl.

'That's wonderful! So why are you looking so sad?'

'Because he told me that he's an atheist. He doesn't even believe there's a Hell!

'Marry him anyway,' said the mother. 'Between the two of us, we'll show him how wrong he is!'

Ken told his friend Mike that the excitement seemed to have gone out of his marriage.

'That often happens when people have been married for fifteen years,' said Mike. 'Have you ever considered having an affair? That might put a bit of sparkle back into your relationship.'

'Are you serious?' asked Ken, dumbfounded. 'No way! I couldn't possibly do that.'

'Get real,' said Mike. 'This is the twenty-first century. These things happen all the time.'

'But what if my wife found out?'

'No problem. Be upfront with her. Tell her about it in advance.'

Overcoming his initial concerns, Ken summoned up the courage to break the news to his wife the next morning while she was reading a magazine over breakfast.

'Honey,' he began hesitantly, 'I don't want you to

take this the wrong way... and please remember that I'm only doing this because I truly, truly love you, otherwise I would never dream of it... but I think maybe... just possibly... having an affair might bring us closer together.'

'Forget it,' said his wife, without even looking up from her magazine. 'I've tried it, and it's never worked.'

Why does a man twist his wedding ring on his finger?
   - He's trying to work out the combination.

A husband and wife were having dinner at a smart restaurant when a stunningly attractive young woman strolled over to their table, gave the husband a big kiss, told him she'd see him later and walked off.

His wife glared at him and demanded, 'Who the hell was that?'

'Oh,' replied the husband nonchalantly, 'that was my mistress.'

'How dare you!' boomed the wife. 'I feel so humiliated – and in public too. I want a divorce.'

'I completely understand,' replied her husband. 'But remember, if you get a divorce, there will be no more shopping trips to Paris, no wintering in the Caribbean, no holidays in the Seychelles and no Ferrari in the garage. But the decision is yours.'

Just then the wife noticed a mutual friend entering the restaurant with a gorgeous woman. 'Who's that woman with Gary?' she asked.

'That's his mistress,' replied her husband.

'Ours is prettier,' said the wife.

What's the only way for a woman to make sure her husband remembers their anniversary?
 - Get married on his birthday.

A woman arrived at the cash desk of a clothes store and reached into her handbag for her purse. As she did so, the sales assistant noticed that there was a TV remote in the woman's handbag.

'Excuse me,' said the sales assistant. 'Do you always carry your TV remote with you when you're shopping?'

'No,' laughed the woman. 'But my husband refused to come shopping with me, so I reckoned this was the most evil thing I could do to him.'

Tom: What did your wife get you for your birthday?
Pete: See that brand-new red Ferrari outside?
Tom: Wow!
Pete: She got me the exact same colour tie.

A wife was showing off her smart new pair of shoes. 'It was very generous of your husband to buy you such expensive shoes,' said a friend.

'He had to,' said the wife. 'I caught him kissing the maid.'

'How awful for you!' said the friend. 'Did you fire her?'

'Certainly not! I still need the matching handbag.'

🐰

A rich man and a poor man were sitting in a bar one night. The poor man asked the rich man what he got his wife for her birthday.

'I got her a brand-new Porsche and a twenty-four-carat diamond ring,' said the rich man.

The poor man, a bit puzzled by this, asked, 'Why did you get her both?'

The rich man replied, 'I got her both because if she doesn't like the ring, she can take it back in her new car and exchange it.'

Then the rich man asked the poor man what he got his wife for her birthday. The poor man answered, 'I got her a scarf and a pair of walking boots.'

Confused, the rich man asked why he chose those items.

The poor man replied, 'Because if she doesn't like the scarf, she can take a hike!'

Did you hear about the X-ray specialist who married one of his patients?

– Everybody wondered what he saw in her.

Three men were sitting in a bar talking about their wives. The first two boasted about how they could get their wives to do anything they wanted. They then turned to the third man who revealed, 'Only yesterday I had my wife crawling towards me on her hands and knees.'

'How did you manage that?' asked the other two, impressed.

He replied, 'Well, I was hiding under the bed and she crawled over and said, "Come out and fight like a man!"'

Despite being high maintenance, Daddy's Little Princess had no shortage of admirers on account of her wealthy background and good looks. She enjoyed using the fact to keep her latest boyfriend on his toes.

'You know,' she told him one day, 'a lot of men are going to be really unhappy when I marry.'

He replied deadpan, 'And just how many men are you intending to marry?'

The guest of honour at a golf club dinner was about to deliver his speech when his wife, who was sitting at the other end of the table, sent him a piece of paper with the word 'KISS' scribbled on it.

A guest seated next to the speaker said, 'Your wife has sent you a KISS before you begin your speech. She must love you very much.'

'You don't know my wife!' said the speaker. 'The letters stand for "Keep It Short, Stupid".'

Genuine Letters to Agony Columns
• I have a man I never could trust. He actually cheats so often that I'm not sure the baby I'm carrying is his.
• I suspected that my husband had been fooling around, and when I confronted him with the evidence he denied everything and said it would never happen again.
• My forty-year-old son has been paying a psychiatrist $50 an hour every week for two-and-a-half years. He must be crazy.
• I was married to Bill for three months and I didn't know he drank until one night he came home sober.
• Do you think it would be all right if I gave my doctor a little gift? I tried for years to get pregnant and couldn't and he finally did it.

A husband was sitting in his back garden looking gloomy. His neighbour called over the fence to ask what the problem was.

'I fell for one of those daft questions women ask,' said the husband, 'and now I'm in the doghouse.'

'What kind of question?' asked the neighbour.

'My wife asked me if I would still love her when she was old, fat and ugly.'

'That's easy,' answered the neighbour. 'You just say, "Of course I will."'

'I know,' sighed the husband. 'That's what I meant to say. But what came out was, "Of course I do."'

One evening after work, a man drove his secretary home after she had drunk a little too much at an office party. Although nothing happened, he decided not to mention it to his wife.

Later that evening, he and his wife were driving to a movie when he spotted a high-heeled shoe under the passenger seat. Pointing to something out of the passenger window in order to distract his wife, he quickly grabbed the shoe and tossed it out of his window.

They arrived at the cinema shortly afterwards and were about to get out of the car when the wife asked, 'Honey, have you seen my other shoe?'

A married couple were shopping in the supermarket when the husband picked up two packs of beer and put them in the trolley.

'What do you think you're doing?' asked the wife.

'They're on special offer,' he explained. 'Only twenty-five dollars for twelve cans.'

'Put them back,' she insisted. 'We can't afford them.'

He did as he was told.

A few aisles later, she picked up a fifty-dollar jar of face cream and put it in the trolley.

'What do you think you're doing?' asked the husband indignantly.

'It's my face cream,' she said. 'It makes me look beautiful.'

He said, 'So do twelve cans of beer and they're half the price!'

'Congratulations, my boy!' said the uncle. 'I'm sure you'll look back on today as the happiest day of your life.'

'But I'm not getting married till tomorrow,' said the young man.

'I know.' The Uncle smiled. 'That's what I mean.'

After celebrating their twenty-fifth wedding anniversary with a romantic candlelit dinner in a restaurant, the wife thanked her husband for a wonderful evening.

'It's not over yet,' he smiled, and back home he presented her with a little black velvet box. She opened it in eager anticipation, but found it contained nothing more exciting than two pills.

'What are these pills?' she asked, puzzled.

'Aspirin.'

'But I don't have a headache.'

'Gotcha!' he cried triumphantly.

What's the difference between a new husband and a new dog?

   – A new dog only takes a couple of months to train.

Why are husbands like lawnmowers?

   – They're hard to get started, they emit foul odours and they don't work half of the time.

Returning home a day early from an out-of-town business trip, a man caught a taxi from the airport in the early hours of the morning. On the cab journey, he confided to the driver that he thought his wife was having an affair. As they pulled up outside his house, the businessman asked the driver, 'Would you come inside with me and be a witness?'

The driver agreed, and they both crept into the bedroom. The man then turned on the lights, pulled back the blanket and, sure enough, his wife was naked in bed with another man.

In a fit of jealousy, the businessman pulled out a gun and threatened to shoot his wife's lover.

'Don't do it,' she begged. 'This man has been very generous. Who do you think paid for the new car I bought you for your birthday? Who do you think paid for our new boat? Who do you think paid for the deposit on this house? He did!'

His mind in turmoil, the husband looked over at the cab driver and asked, 'What would you do in a case like this?'

The cabbie said, 'I think I'd cover him up before he catches cold.'

'Honey,' said the husband to his wife, 'I've invited a friend home for supper.'

'What?!' she yelled. 'Are you crazy? The house is a mess, there's a pile of dirty dishes in the sink and I really can't be bothered to cook a fancy meal.'

'I know all that,' he said.

'Then why did you invite a friend for supper?'

'Because the poor fool is thinking about getting married.'

A wife asked her husband, 'What do you like most about me – my pretty face or my sexy body?'
He looked her up and down and replied, 'Your sense of humour.'

Arriving home from a shopping trip, a wife was horrified to find her husband in bed with a young woman. Just as the wife was about to storm out of the house, he stopped her and said, 'Before you leave, I want you to hear how all this came about. You see, I was driving home when I saw this poor young woman looking hungry, tired and bedraggled. So I brought her back here and made her a meal from the minced beef you had forgotten about. All she had on her feet were some battered old trainers, so I gave her a pair of perfectly good shoes that you had discarded because they had gone out of style. She was cold so I also gave her a sweater that I bought you for your birthday but which you never wore because you didn't like the shade of green. Her jeans were worn out so in the bottom of your wardrobe I found a pair of yours that are too small for you. Then, when she was about to leave the house, she paused and asked, "Is there anything else your wife doesn't use any more?"'

A man and his wife were sitting in the living room when he turned to her and said, 'Just so you know, I never want to live in a vegetative state dependent on some machine. If that ever happens, just pull the plug.'

'OK,' said his wife – and she got up and unplugged the TV.

Two newlyweds soon realized that their marriage wasn't working and filed for divorce. The judge asked them what the problem was.

The husband replied, 'In the five weeks that we've been together, we haven't been able to agree on a single thing.'

The judge turned to the wife, 'Have you anything to say?'

She answered, 'It's been six weeks, your honour.'

When a man opens the door of his car for his wife, you can be sure of one thing: either the car is new or the wife is.

A young couple rushed into a city church and said to the minister, 'We want to get married right away. Here are all our papers, and these people are our witnesses. Can you do a quick service?'

Although taken aback by the urgency, the minister duly conducted a short service and pocketed his fee. But afterwards he felt the need to say to the groom, 'Isn't there a proverb about marrying in haste? Why are you two in such a hurry?'

Dragging his bride after him, the groom ran out into the street and shouted back to the minister, 'We're double-parked!'

Instead of coming home from work one Friday afternoon, a man blew his weekly pay cheque by staying out with his friends all weekend and partying. When he finally went home on the Sunday night, his wife was understandably furious. She berated him for over an hour before screaming, 'How would you like it if you didn't see me for two whole days?'

'As a matter of fact that would suit me just fine!' he replied defiantly.

So he didn't see his wife on Monday or Tuesday, but by Wednesday the swelling had gone down enough so that he could just see her out of the corner of his left eye.

A man said to his friend, 'I'm in big trouble. I got a letter from a guy who said he'd break both my legs if I didn't stop seeing his wife.'

'Right,' said the friend. 'I guess you'll have to stop seeing her.'

'That won't be easy.'

'Why? You like her that much?'

'No, it's not that. He didn't sign his name.'

A couple's marriage nearly broke up because of the presence in their home of old Aunt Agnes. For seventeen long years she lived with them, always bad-tempered, always demanding, right up until the day she finally died.

On the way back from the cemetery, the husband confessed to his wife, 'Darling, if I didn't love you so much I don't think I could have put up with having your Aunt Agnes in the house all those years.'

His wife looked at him in horror. '*My* Aunt Agnes?' she cried. 'I thought she was *your* Aunt Agnes!'

After twenty-five years of marriage, a husband looked at his wife one day and said, 'Twenty-five years ago we had a cheap apartment, a cheap car and slept on a sofa bed, but I didn't care because every night I got to sleep with a sexy twenty-eight-year-old blonde. Now we have a nice house, nice car and a big bed, but I'm sleeping with a fifty-three-year-old woman who, to be brutally honest, has let herself go.'

His wife replied calmly, 'Then why don't you go out and find yourself a sexy twenty-eight-year-old blonde? And if you do, I'll make sure that once again you'll be living in a cheap apartment, driving a cheap car and sleeping on a sofa bed!'

If Men Planned Weddings
• All wedding dresses would be at least three inches above the knee and made of leather.
• It would be perfectly acceptable for the groom to wear T-shirt and jeans.
• No weddings would take place during the football season.
• Wedding vows would mention sex and cooking specifically but would omit all that stuff about forsaking all others.
• Ceremonies would be short and honeymoons long.
• The wedding cake would be a pizza.
• It would be obligatory for the best man to sleep with the chief bridesmaid.
• More money would be spent on the stag night than on the wedding because strippers don't come cheap.
• Instead of a sit-down meal or a buffet, there would be a hog roast and buckets of chicken.

A man asked his wife what she would like for her fiftieth birthday, and she said, 'I'd love to be eight again.'

So on the morning of her birthday he took her off to an amusement park and made her go on all the rides – the rollercoaster, Wall of Death, water slide, the lot.

Six hours later, she staggered out of the park, her head reeling and her stomach all over the place. Then he took her to McDonald's for a Happy Meal and finally to the movies to watch the latest Disney adventure, accompanied by a giant tub of popcorn.

When she got home, she collapsed exhausted on the bed.

'So,' he said, 'how did it feel to be eight again?'

'You idiot!' she exclaimed. 'I meant my dress size!'

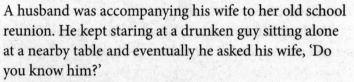

A husband was accompanying his wife to her old school reunion. He kept staring at a drunken guy sitting alone at a nearby table and eventually he asked his wife, 'Do you know him?'

'Yes,' she replied. 'That's my old boyfriend. I understand he started drinking right after we split up all those years ago, and apparently he hasn't been sober for the forty years since.'

'Good heavens!' exclaimed the husband. 'You wouldn't think someone could go on celebrating that long!'

If you want to drive your wife crazy, don't talk in your sleep – just smile.

Two deaf men met in the library and began talking about being out late the night before. The first man signed to his friend, 'My wife was asleep when I got home so I was able to sneak into bed and not get into trouble.'

The second deaf man signed back, 'You were lucky. My wife was wide awake, waiting up for me in bed, and when I walked in she started swearing at me and giving me hell for being out so late.'

The first deaf man asked, 'So what did you do?' The second man replied, 'I turned out the light.'

A man and a woman who had never met before found themselves sharing a cabin on an overnight sleeper train. After the initial awkwardness, he went in the upper berth and she went in the lower bunk.

In the middle of the night, he leaned down, tapped her on the shoulder and said, 'I'm sorry to bother you, but I'm really cold, so I was wondering whether you could possibly get me another blanket.'

The woman replied coyly, 'I have a better idea. Just for tonight, let's pretend that we are married.'

'That sounds great,' said the man, preparing to climb down to join her.

'Good,' said the woman. 'Get your own bloody blanket!'

Husband: My wife's a peach.
Friend: So is mine – but only because she has a heart of stone.

Despite being granted a divorce on the grounds of her husband's infidelity, a woman was forced to move out of the house she had lovingly looked after for twenty-eight years. She spent four whole days packing her belongings into boxes, crates and suitcases, and then on the fifth day the removal men came to collect her things. That evening, she sat alone in the house for the last time, preparing herself a final farewell meal of prawns and caviar, which she ate by candlelight at their beautiful dining-room table. She was sad but bitter too, and at the end of the meal she went into every room and placed a few half-eaten prawn shells dipped in caviar into the hollows of the curtain rods. She then tidied up the kitchen and left.

When the husband moved back in with his new girlfriend, all was bliss for the first few days. Then slowly the house began to acquire a strange smell. They tried everything to get rid of it – cleaning the place from top to bottom. Vents were checked for dead rodents and carpets were steam-cleaned. Air fresheners were hung everywhere. Pest exterminators were called in to set off gas canisters, which made such a mess the couple had to move out for a few days and replace all their expensive wool carpets. But still nothing worked.

After a while, friends stopped coming to visit, repairmen refused to work in the house and the maid quit, fearing for her health.

Eventually, they could bear the stench no longer and decided to put the house up for sale. But prospective buyers were immediately put off by the smell and, despite the price being greatly reduced, several months later they had still not managed to sell it. Things were so bad that they had to borrow a large sum of money from the bank in order to purchase a new home.

Word of their misfortune reached the ears of his ex-wife, who called to ask him how he was doing. When he relayed the saga of the rotting house, she listened politely and said that she missed her old home terribly. She suggested that she would even be willing to reduce her divorce settlement in exchange for getting her beloved house back.

The husband jumped at the idea and made sure that all the necessary paperwork for the transaction went through swiftly. With the sale completed, he and his girlfriend congratulated themselves on finally finding a mug willing to take the horrible, stinking house off their hands and they smiled smugly as they watched the removal company pack up everything to take to their new home.

And, just to spite his ex-wife, they even took the curtain rods!

MONEY

A teenage boy went off to university, but about a third of the way through the semester, he had foolishly squandered all the money his parents had given him. Desperate to get extra funds out of his father, he came up with a devious plan.

Phoning home one weekend, he said, 'Dad, you won't believe the educational opportunities that are available at this university! Why, they've even got a course here that will teach Buddy how to talk!'

'They can teach a dog to talk? That's incredible!' said the gullible father. 'How do I enrol him on the course?'

'Just send him down here with $1,000,' said the son, 'and I'll make sure he gets on the course.'

So the father sent the dog and $1,000, but about two-thirds of the way through the semester, that money had also run out. The boy called his father again.

'How's Buddy doing?' asked the father.

'Awesome, Dad. He's talking great. But you just won't believe this; they've had such amazing results with the talking dogs' course that they're starting up a new one to teach the animals how to read!'

'Read?' echoed the father. 'No kidding! What do I have to do to get him on that course?'

'Just send $2,000 and I'll get him on the course.'

So the father sent the money, but at the end of the semester, the boy was faced with a problem: how to conceal from his father the fact that the dog could neither talk nor read. So the son decided to take drastic action and shot the dog. When he arrived home for vacation, his father was waiting expectantly.

'Where's Buddy?' asked the father. 'I can't wait to hear him talk or listen to him read something.'

'Dad,' said the boy solemnly, 'I've got some bad news. This morning when I stepped out of the shower, Buddy was in the living room reading the morning paper, like he usually does. Then suddenly he turned to me and asked, 'So, is your dad still messing around with that little blonde at number thirty-seven?'

The father's face turned red with rage and he yelled, 'I

hope you shot that lying dog!'

'I sure did, Dad.'

'That's my boy!'

What's the best way to keep your bills down?

– Use a paperweight.

A tramp stopped a man in the street and said, 'Give me ten bucks till payday.'

The man said, 'When's payday?'

'I don't know,' said the tramp. 'You're the one who's working.'

A city businessman moved to the country and bought a donkey from a farmer for a hundred dollars. The farmer agreed to deliver the donkey the next day, but when he drove up in his truck, he had some bad news.

'Sorry,' he said. 'The donkey has died.'

'Well, just give me my money back.'

'I can't; I've spent it.'

'OK then, just unload the donkey.'

'What are you going to do with him?' asked the farmer.

'I'm going to raffle him off.'

'You can't raffle off a dead donkey!'

'Sure I can,' insisted the businessman. 'I just won't tell anyone he's dead.'

The next month, the farmer met up with the businessman again and asked, 'What happened with the dead donkey?'

'I raffled him off – just like I said I would. I sold five hundred tickets at two dollars apiece and made a profit of nine hundred and ninety-eight dollars.'

'Didn't anyone complain?'

'Only the guy who won. So I gave him his two dollars back.'

Why did the man put his money in the freezer?
  – He wanted to cold hard cash.

MUSIC

An elderly lady had always wanted to learn to play a musical instrument so for her sixty-fifth birthday her husband bought her a grand piano.

A few weeks later, their neighbours saw the husband in the street. 'How's the piano playing coming along?' they asked.

'Oh,' he said, 'we took it back to the store. I persuaded her to switch to a clarinet instead.'

'Why?' asked the neighbours.

'Because she can't sing whilst playing the clarinet!'

A resident oboist at the opera house was offered a fantastic gig eighty miles away on the same day that he was due to play with the opera house orchestra. After his attempts to find a replacement professional musician proved unsuccessful, he begged his housekeeper to take his place. 'I'll give you my spare oboe,' he said. 'All you have to do is copy what the guy on the oboe next to you is doing. It will be fine.'

The next morning, he asked the housekeeper how the opera house performance went.

'It was a disaster,' she said. 'Your colleague also sent his housekeeper to replace him.'

What's the difference between a viola and an anchor?
- You tie a rope to the anchor before you throw it overboard.

A girl had learned to play the piano at a very young age, and by the time she was in her late teens it had become one of the great passions in her life. At great expense to her parents, she studied at the Royal College of Music, where she excelled. Her ambition was to play the piano professionally and, because she also loved to travel, she decided to apply to join the army as a musician. The demanding series of selection interviews included written tests and no fewer than five arduous piano-playing demonstrations. Eventually, she was accepted and was so thrilled that she happily signed up for overseas duty.

Her first posting was to Afghanistan. In the first letter she received from her parents, they asked how she felt about finally being able to play the piano for a living. She wrote back, 'Things have changed a little. It's impossible to drag a piano all over the war zone, so I am now playing the cymbals.'

Why was the man in no fit state to play his stringed instrument?

  – He was harpist.

A young man bought his mother a CD player and some CDs, and she was thrilled to discover that she no longer needed to rewind or fast-forward tapes or move the needle on her record player. Knowing that she wasn't technologically aware, he called her a few days later to ask how she was getting on with the new gadget.

'It's wonderful,' she said. 'I listened to Fleetwood Mac this morning.'

'The whole CD?' he asked.

'No,' she replied. 'Just one side.'

Musician: Did you hear my last recital?
Friend: I hope so.

A woman answered the door of her house to find a workman standing on the front porch. 'I'm the piano tuner,' he announced.

'But I didn't send for a piano tuner,' she said.

'I know,' he said, 'but your neighbours did.'

Why was the guitar player worried?
   – He was always fretting about something.

A man walked into a bar with his pet octopus. He sat the octopus down on a stool and told everyone in the bar that the octopus was so talented it could play any musical instrument in the world. When people started to laugh, the man said he would wager fifty dollars that the octopus could play any instrument provided.

Immediately a challenger walked up with a guitar and put it down next to the octopus, who picked it up and started playing better than Jimi Hendrix. Stunned, the challenger handed over fifty dollars. Then another man handed the octopus a trumpet. The octopus played better than Miles Davis, and the challenger paid up his fifty dollars.

At that point a Scotsman appeared with a set of bagpipes and handed the instrument to the octopus, who fumbled with it for a minute before putting it back down. 'What's the matter?' asked the Scotsman. 'Can't you play it?'

'Play it?' said the octopus. 'I'm going to shag it as soon as I can get its pyjamas off!'

OLD AGE

Twin sisters at a retirement home were celebrating their 100th birthdays. To mark the occasion, the local newspaper sent along a photographer to take some pictures. One of the twins, Edith, was a bit deaf but the other, Joan, could hear quite well.

First, the photographer asked the sisters to sit on the sofa.

Edith called to her twin, 'What did he say?'

'He wants us to sit over there on the sofa,' said Joan.

So they sat on the sofa.

'Now, move a little closer together, please,' said the photographer.

'What did he say?' shouted Edith.

'He wants us to squeeze together a little,' replied Joan.
So they huddled up next to each other.

'Now, just hold that pose for a few seconds,' said the photographer. 'I've got to focus.'

'What did he say?' yelled Edith.

'He says he's gonna focus,' answered Joan.

'Oh, my goodness!' shrieked Edith. 'Both of us?'

When a ninety-year-old man married a twenty-year-old girl, the wedding guests privately feared that the wedding night might prove fatal because he was a frail old man and she was a vivacious young woman. But the next morning everyone was surprised to see the bride come down the main stairwell of the hotel very gingerly, step by step, and painfully bow-legged. Eventually, she managed to hobble to the front desk.

Seeing the state of her, the clerk asked the bride, 'What on earth happened to you?'

'It's my husband!' she gasped. 'What a night! It's a wonder I'm still alive! When he told me that he'd been saving up for seventy years, I thought he meant his money!'

A salesman was calling door-to-door, trying to sell vacuum cleaners. When he called at one house, the old lady who lived there told him bluntly that she was not interested and slammed the door in his face. But to her surprise, the door didn't close and instead bounced back open. So she tried for a second time, with more force, but the door still wouldn't close and bounced back open again.

Convinced that the salesman was deliberately putting his foot in the door to prevent her shutting it, she reared back to give the door an almighty slam that would finally teach him a lesson.

But as she went to do so, the salesman interrupted: 'Madam, before you do that again, I think you ought to move your cat.'

Seeing her friend Jenny wearing a new locket, Susan asked if it contained a memento.

'Yes,' said Jenny, 'it holds a lock of my husband's hair.'

'But David's still alive…'

'I know,' said Jenny, 'but his hair has gone.'

Senior Citizens' Alphabet

A for arthritis, **B** for bad back, **C** is for chest pains. Perhaps cardiac?

D is for dental decay and decline, **E** is for eyesight – can't read that top line.

F is for fissures and fluid retention, **G** is for gas (which I'd rather not mention).

H is high blood pressure (I'd rather have low), **I** for incisions with scars you can show.

J is for joints that now fail to flex,

L for libido – what happened to sex? Wait! I forgot about **K**!

K is for my knees that crack when they're bent, (please forgive me, my Memory ain't worth a cent).

N for neurosis, pinched nerves and stiff neck, **O** is for osteo- and all bones that crack. **P** for prescriptions, I have quite a few – Give me another pill; I'll be good as new!

Q is for queasiness. Fatal or flu? **R** is for reflux – one meal turns into two.

S is for sleepless nights, counting my fears, **T** for tinnitus – I hear bells in my ears.

U is for urinary: problems with flow, **V** is for vertigo, that's 'dizzy', you know.

W is worry, now what's going 'round? **X** is for X ray – and what might be found.

Y for another year I've left behind, **Z** is for zest that I still have my mind.

Have survived all the symptoms my body's deployed, and kept twenty-six doctors gainfully employed!

An elderly spinster called a lawyer's office and asked him to visit her with a view to preparing her will. When he arrived, she told him, 'I have lived a very reclusive life. I hardly ever leave the house, and so people tend not to notice me. However, when I die I would like to be noticed for once. Through years of careful saving I have built up fifty thousand dollars in the bank, and I would like forty-five thousand of that to be spent on my funeral so that people around here will remember me for years to come. I want an ornate coach, black horses and the most lavish show that my money can buy.'

'For that amount of money, you'll be able to have the grandest funeral in town,' said the lawyer. 'It will almost be like a state occasion. And what do you want to do with the other five thousand dollars?'

The spinster replied, 'I have lived a very sheltered life. I have never married and have never even slept with a man. So before I die, I'd like you to arrange for a man to sleep with me.'

'This is a most unusual request,' said the lawyer, 'but I'll see what I can do to arrange it and get back to you.

That evening the lawyer told his wife about the eccentric spinster's strange request. The wife thought how five thousand dollars could buy that nice new three-piece suite she had been admiring in the store and eventually she persuaded her husband to provide the service himself. She said, 'I'll drive you over tomorrow morning and wait in the car.'

So the next morning she drove him over to the spinster's house and waited in the car. An hour and a half later, when he had still not reappeared, she sounded the horn. The upstairs bedroom window opened, the lawyer stuck his head out and yelled, 'Pick me up tomorrow! She's going to let the council bury her!'

Two elderly widows, Ethel and Sadie, were talking. Ethel said, 'I'm going on a date next week with that Maurice Robertson from the lunch club.'

'Well,' said Sadie, 'I went out with him last month, and I could tell you a few tales about him. He turned up at my apartment immaculately dressed and carrying a huge bouquet of flowers for me. He then ordered a limousine to take me to this beautiful restaurant, and after the most fantastic dinner we went to see a show. He was a perfect gentleman until we got back to my apartment and he turned into an animal! He tore off my expensive new dress and had wild sex with me twice.'

'Oh, dear,' said Ethel, 'do you think I should cancel our date?'

'No,' replied Sadie. 'I'm just saying wear an old dress.'

A husband was so impressed by the meat dish served for dinner that at the end of the meal he asked his wife, 'What did you marinate this in?'

She immediately went into a long explanation about how much she loved him, how she cherished their forty years together and how she could never imagine life without him. Seeing the puzzled expression on his face, she said, 'What did you ask me?'

Hearing his answer, she chuckled and said, 'Sorry, I thought you asked me if I would marry you again!'

As she left to go into the kitchen, he called out, 'Well, would you marry me again?'

She replied, 'Vinegar and barbecue sauce.'

An old man was asleep in his chair one afternoon when he was awoken by the sound of the doorbell. He shuffled to the door and when he opened it, he saw a beautiful young woman standing there.

'Oh, I'm so sorry,' she said. 'I'm at the wrong house.'

The old man smiled. 'Oh, no, sweetheart, you're at the right house... but you're forty years too late!'

Three old men were sitting on a park bench. The first said, 'It used to take me five minutes to get here but today – half an hour. At eighty-five years, my legs are letting me down.'

The second said, 'Legs, that's nothing! I used to read the newspaper without glasses, but today even with glasses I can't read it. At ninety years, it's my eyes that are letting me down.'

The third scoffed, 'Eyes and legs, that's nothing! When I went home yesterday evening after I left you, I looked at my wife doing the washing-up, felt the urge and said to her, "Let's go and make love." She replied, "You've already done it once today." At ninety-five years, my memory's letting me down!'

Signs That You're Getting Old
• You forget names, but it doesn't matter because other people forget they even know you.
• You sleep better in a comfy chair in front of a blaring TV than you do in bed.
• You read seventy pages into a book before you realize you've read it before.
• Now that you finally afford expensive jewellery, it's not safe to wear it anywhere.
• You realize you're never going to be really good at anything, especially golf.
• Your kids are becoming you, and you don't like them. But your grandchildren are perfect.

- You can have a night out with the boys and be home by 9 p.m.
- Everybody around you seems to whisper.
- You have a better chance of losing your keys than of losing weight.
- You use more four-letter words, like 'what?' and 'when?'

An elderly man had become so hard of hearing that he decided to buy a hearing aid, but he couldn't afford to spend much money. 'How much do they cost?' he asked the sales assistant.

'Anything from five dollars to five hundred dollars.'

'Can I see the five-dollar model?' said the old man.

The sales assistant put the device around the man's neck, and said, 'You just stick this button in your ear and run this little string down to your pocket.'

'How does it work?' asked the old man.

'For five dollars, it doesn't work,' said the sales assistant. 'But when people see it on you, they'll talk louder!'

A husband wanted his eighty-year-old wife dead and asked a hired assassin how he would do it.

'I would shoot off her left nipple,' said the assassin.

The husband threw up his hands in horror, exclaiming, 'I want her dead – not kneecapped!'

Sophie and Jessica, two elderly widows in a Florida retirement home, were curious about the latest arrival in their building – a quiet, nice-looking gentleman who liked to keep himself to himself.

One day, Sophie said, 'Jessica, you know I'm shy. Why don't you go over to him in the garden and find out a little about him? He looks so lonely.'

Jessica agreed, and later that day she walked over to him in the garden and said, 'Excuse me, mister. I hope I'm not prying, but my friend and I were wondering why you looked so lonely.'

'Of course I'm lonely,' he said. 'I've spent the past twenty years in prison.'

'You're kidding! What for?'

'For killing my third wife. I strangled her.'

'What happened to your second wife?'

'I poisoned her.'

'And, if I may ask, what happened to your first wife?'

'We had a fight and she fell off a building.'

'Oh, my!' said Jessica. Then, turning to her friend on

the other side of the garden, she yelled, 'Yoo hoo, Sophie. He's single.'

Two senior ladies who were keen social rivals met at a party.

'Are those real pearls?' sneered one.

'They certainly are,' replied the other.

'Of course,' said the first, 'the only way I could tell for sure would be for me to bite them.'

'Yes, my dear, but to do that you would need real teeth.'

An old man went to the doctor for his annual medical check-up. He told the doctor, 'I'm getting really forgetful. I forget where I live, I forget where I've parked my car, and I go into shops and I can't remember what it is that I want. And when I do get to the checkout, I realize that I've forgotten my wallet. It's getting pretty bad, doc. What can I do?'

The doctor thought for a moment and said, 'Pay me in advance.'

Maurice and Kitty were sitting down to breakfast, listening to the weather report on the radio. The announcer said, 'There will be five inches of snow today, and an emergency has been declared. You must park your car on the odd-numbered side of the street.'

'Oh, OK,' sighed Maurice, getting up from his coffee.

The next day at breakfast, the radio announcer said, 'There will be eight inches of snow today, and another emergency has been declared. Please park your car on the even-numbered side of the street.'

Again, Maurice sighed, 'OK,' and got up from his coffee.

The following day at breakfast, the radio announcer said, 'There will be twelve inches of snow today, and another emergency has been declared. Please park your car...' Just then there was a power cut and Maurice didn't hear the rest of the instructions. He turned to Kitty and said in a worried tone, 'What am I going to do now, Kitty?'

Kitty replied, 'Oh, just leave the car in the garage today.'

289

Two old men were sitting in a bar discussing their sex lives. The first said, 'Last night, I asked Maureen if we could do it doggy-style for a change.'

'And did you?' asked the second.

'I'll say we did it doggy-style! I sat up and begged, she rolled over and played dead!'

A couple were having a special dinner to celebrate their golden wedding anniversary. In the course of the meal, the old man leaned forward and said softly to his wife, 'Dear, there is something that I must ask you. It has always concerned me that our ninth child never quite looked like the rest of our children. Now, I want to assure you that these fifty years have been the most wonderful experience I could have ever hoped for and your answer cannot destroy my precious memories of our life together. But I need to know: did he have a different father?'

The wife hung her head, unable to look her husband in the eye. She paused for a moment and then confessed, 'Yes. Yes, he did.'

The old man was shaken by the revelation. The reality of what his wife was admitting hit him harder than he had expected. With a tear in his eye he asked,

'Who was he? Who was the father?'

Again his wife looked ashamed, but said nothing at first as she tried to muster the courage to tell the truth to her husband. Then finally she took a deep breath and said, 'You.'

An elderly couple moved into a house that needed a lot of work doing to it before it met their standards. The wife was particularly unhappy and complained endlessly to her husband about the state of the place. 'The wallpaper in the lounge is peeling, there's mildew around the kitchen windows and worst of all there are no curtains in the bathroom. So the neighbours can see me every time I take a bath.'

'Don't worry,' replied her husband wearily. 'If the neighbours do see you, they'll buy curtains!'

A deaf old lady went to the doctor to find out whether there was any risk of her getting pregnant again.

He told her, 'Mrs Davies, you're seventy-two. Whilst one can never rule out an act of God, if you were to have a baby it would be a miracle.'

When she got home, her husband asked her what the doctor had said.

'I didn't quite catch it all,' she admitted, 'but it sounded a bit fishy; something about an act of cod, and if I had a baby it would be a mackerel.'

A 105-year-old man was asked by a television crew what the secret of his longevity was.

'It's because I gave up sex,' he replied.

'When did you give up sex?' asked the reporter.

'Ten years ago.'

'I see,' said the reporter. 'And would you mind telling me why you gave up sex?'

'I had to. I like older women!'

It was the talk of the town when an eighty-year-old man married a twenty-year-old girl – even more so when nine months later she went into hospital to give birth. The nurse congratulated the old man on his energy and asked him how he was still able to father children at his age.

'Simple,' he said. 'You've got to keep that old motor running!'

The following year, the young wife gave birth again. The nurse said to the old man, 'You're amazing! I don't know what your secret is!'

'Well,' he said, 'you've just got to keep that old motor running!'

A year later, the young wife gave birth to a third child. Spotting the same nurse at the hospital, the old man grinned. 'See what I mean about keeping that old motor running?'

'I think it could be time to change your oil,' replied the nurse, 'because this one's black!'

🐻

A group of fifteen-year-old schoolgirls decided to meet up for dinner. They discussed where to eat and finally agreed on the Clock Tower Café because it was cheap and the cutest boy in class lived nearby.

Ten years later, the same girlfriends – now twenty-five – discussed where to meet for dinner. Finally, they agreed to meet at the Clock Tower Café because there was no cover charge, the beer was cheap, the band was good, and there were plenty of good-looking men.

Ten years later, the same girlfriends – now thirty-five – debated where to meet for dinner. Finally, they decided to go to the Clock Tower Café because it served good wine, it was near the gym and if they got there after eight there would be no children running around.

Ten years later, the same girlfriends – now forty-five – discussed where to meet for dinner. Finally, they agreed on the Clock Tower Café because the martinis were big and the waiters wore tight jeans.

Ten years later, the same girlfriends – now fifty-five – discussed where to meet for dinner. Finally, they agreed on the Clock Tower Café because the air conditioning was efficient and the fish was good for their cholesterol.

Ten years later, the same girlfriends – now sixty-five – debated where to meet for dinner. Finally, they decided on the Clock Tower Café because they could get special rates if they went early, the lighting was good and the menu was in large print.

Ten years later, the same girlfriends – now seventy-five – discussed where to meet for dinner. Finally, they agreed on the Clock Tower Café because it had wheelchair access and the food wasn't too spicy.

Ten years later, the same girlfriends – now eighty-five – discussed where to meet for dinner. Finally, they agreed on the Clock Tower Café because they had never been there before.

POLITICIANS

As the band started to play at an embassy function, a politician who had been drinking all evening staggered over and said, 'Beautiful lady in red, will you waltz with me?'

'Certainly not,' came the reply. 'First, you are drunk. Second, it is not a waltz but the Venezuelan national anthem. And third, I am not a beautiful lady in red, but the papal nuncio.'

Husband-and-wife politicians were staying at an expensive hotel while attending a top-level international arms conference. The wife was concerned about privacy and feared that, given the sensitive nature of the conference, their room might be bugged. To ease her fears, the husband searched the room thoroughly for listening devices, looking behind curtains and pictures and under the bed. Finally, under the rug he found a disc with four screws. He immediately got a knife, unscrewed the screws and tossed them and the disc out of the window.

The next morning, the hotel manager asked them whether their room was OK. 'Why do you ask?' said the husband suspiciously.

'Well,' said the manager, 'the room under you complained of the chandelier falling on them.'

Two politicians were locked in a heated debate on television. Finally, one of them yelled at the other, 'What about the powerful interest that controls you?'

The other politician screamed back, 'You leave my wife out of this!'

While walking down the street one day, a leading Republican politician was hit by a truck and died. His soul arrived in Heaven and was met by St Peter at the Pearly Gates.

'Welcome to Heaven,' said St Peter. 'Before you settle in, it seems there is a problem. You see, we seldom see a high-ranking politician around these parts, so we're not sure what to do with you.'

'No problem,' barked the Republican. 'Just let me in.'

'Well,' said St Peter, 'I'd like to but I have orders from higher up. What we'll do is have you spend one day in Hell and one in Heaven. Then you can choose where to spend eternity.'

'Really, I've made up my mind. I want to be in Heaven,' said the Republican.

'I'm sorry, but we have our rules,' St Peter insisted. And with that, St Peter escorted the Republican to the elevator and he went down, down, down, all the way to Hell. The doors opened and he found himself in the middle of a green golf course. In the distance was a club and standing in front of it were all his friends and other politicians who had worked with him. Everyone was very happy and wearing evening dress. They ran to greet him, hug him and reminisce about the good times they'd had while getting rich at expense of the people. Then they played a friendly game of golf before dining on lobster and caviar. Also present was the Devil (a Republican too), a very friendly guy who enjoyed dancing and telling jokes.

They were all having such a good time that the Republican politician lost track of the time and before long it was time to go. Everyone gave him a big hug and waved while the elevator rose. The elevator went up, up, up, and the door reopened in Heaven, where St Peter was waiting for him.

'Now it's time to visit Heaven,' said St Peter. So for the next twenty-four hours, the senior Republican joined a group of contented souls moving from cloud to cloud, playing the harp and singing. It was pleasant enough, but the Republican missed his friends. Eventually, after what seemed like a lifetime, the twenty-four hours were up and St Peter reappeared.

'Well then,' he said, 'you've spent a day in Hell and another in Heaven. Now choose your eternity.'

The politician reflected for a minute, and then answered diplomatically, 'Well, I would never have thought it – I mean, Heaven has been delightful, but I think I would be better off in Hell.'

So, St Peter escorted him to the elevator and he went down, down, down, all the way to Hell. Now the doors of the elevator opened and he was in the middle of a barren land covered with waste and garbage. He saw all his friends, dressed in rags, picking up the trash and putting it in black bags. The Devil came over to the Republican.

'I don't understand,' stammered the Republican. 'Yesterday, I was here and there was a golf course and a club and we ate lobster and caviar and danced and had a great time. Now all I see is a wasteland full of garbage and my friends look miserable.'

The Devil looked at him, smiled and said, 'Ah, but yesterday, we were campaigning. Today, you voted for us!'

A little girl asked her father, 'Do all fairy tales begin with "Once upon a time"?'

'No,' replied the father. 'Some begin with "If I am elected".'

A team of aliens landed in Washington, DC, on the first official state visit from Mars. They were honoured at a banquet at the White House and spent hours talking to senior Republicans and Democrats. After a day and a night of discussing various issues with the politicians, the aliens returned to their home planet. 'Bad news,' said the returning alien leader to his boss. 'We wasted all that time and we still don't know if there is intelligent life on Earth.'

Two rival politicians were campaigning in the same small town, shaking hands, kissing babies, posing for photos and making empty promises. After an hour of them working the streets, it suddenly started to pour with rain. One of the candidates fled to take shelter in a nearby restaurant but his opponent stayed out and continued to chat to passers-by despite the awful weather.

One local said, 'That man's persistence sure makes it easy to know who to vote for.'

'Yep,' agreed another. 'I can't see myself voting for any man who hasn't the good sense to come in out of the rain.'

The year is 2016 and Naomi Rosenberg has just been elected the first woman President of the United States. Shortly after the election, she rang her mother in Florida and said, 'I hope you'll be coming to my inauguration?'

'I don't think so,' said her mother. 'It's a long drive,

your father's back is playing him up again and, anyway, neither of us is as young as we used to be.'

'Don't worry, Mom. I'll send Air Force One to pick you up and take you home, and a limousine will collect you from your door. You'll hardly have to walk anywhere.'

'I'm not sure. Besides, it will be such a fancy occasion. I haven't got anything to wear.'

'No problem, Mom. I'll pay for you to have a dress made by one of the world's leading designers.'

'That's all very well, but you know I can't stomach the rich food that you and your friends eat. I'd be up with indigestion for weeks afterwards.'

'I can sort it, Mom. I'll have a special menu drawn up just for you. Please, say you'll come. It would mean so much to me.'

Reluctantly, the mother agreed, and was in the front row as Naomi Rosenberg was sworn in as the first woman President of the United States. Turning to the senator sitting next to her, the mother said, 'See that woman over there with her hand on the Bible, becoming President of the United States?'

'Yes, I do,' said the senator.

'Her brother's a doctor.'

PSYCHIATRISTS

A psychiatrist was doing the rounds in a mental hospital when a patient entered the ward, waving his arms about and making beeping noises.

'Excuse me,' said the psychiatrist. 'What are you doing?'

'I'm driving my car,' he replied cheerily. 'Beep, beep!'

'But you're in a mental hospital,' explained the psychiatrist. 'You're not in a car.'

'Don't tell him that,' cried one of the other patients. 'He pays me ten dollars a week to wash it.'

A man told a psychiatrist that he had a phobia about answering the phone. The psychiatrist listened patiently to the man's fears, gave him some advice and asked him to come back in a month.

A month later, the man returned for his follow-up appointment.

'So how are your problems with the phone?' asked the psychiatrist.

'I think you've cured me,' said the man. 'Now I answer it whether it rings or not.'

A young boy was so obsessed with cricket that his parents sent him to see a psychiatrist. The boy confessed, 'All I ever do is dream about playing for England at Lord's.'

'Really?' said the psychiatrist. 'Don't you ever dream about girls?'

'What, and lose my turn to bat?'

What happened when a car mechanic went to see a psychiatrist?

- He lay down under the couch.

A young man went to a psychiatrist to seek a cure for an eating and sleeping disorder.

He told the psychiatrist, 'Every thought I have turns to my mother. Her voice is in my head all the time, night and day. As soon as I fall asleep and start to dream, I wake up so upset that all I can do is go downstairs and eat a slice of toast.'

The psychiatrist said, 'What, just one slice of toast for a growing boy like you?'

Two psychiatrists were cycling along the road when one fell and badly injured himself. As the poor man lay writhing in agony on the ground with blood pouring from his wounds, the other psychiatrist said, 'Do you want to talk about it?'

Three patients in a mental institution were preparing to be examined by the head psychiatrist. If the patients passed the exam, they would be free to leave the hospital; if not, they would be detained indefinitely.

The doctor took the three to the top of a diving board overlooking an empty swimming pool, and asked the first patient to jump.

The first patient jumped head first into the empty pool and broke both arms.

Then, the second patient jumped and broke both legs.

Finally, it was the turn of the third patient. He looked anxiously over the side but refused to jump.

'Congratulations!' said the psychiatrist. 'You're a free man. Just tell me why you didn't jump.'

The third patient answered, 'Well, doctor, I can't swim.'

Did you hear about the paranoid man with low self-esteem?

– He thought nobody important was out to get him.

A woman went to see a psychiatrist. 'Doctor, I want to talk to you about my husband. He thinks he's a refrigerator.'

'That's not so bad,' said the psychiatrist. 'It's a fairly harmless contraption.'

'Maybe,' she said. 'But he sleeps with his mouth open and the light keeps me awake.'

REDNECKS

After having their tenth child, a redneck couple decided that was enough because they could not afford a larger trailer home. So the husband went to his doctor and told him that he and his wife didn't want to have any more children. The doctor told him that there was a procedure called a vasectomy that could fix the problem. The doctor instructed him to go home, get a firecracker, light it, put it in a beer can, then hold the can up to his ear and count to ten.

The redneck said to the doctor, 'I may not be the smartest man, but I don't see how putting a firecracker in a beer can next to my ear is going to help me.'

So the couple drove to get a second opinion. The

second doctor was just about to tell them about the medical procedure for a vasectomy when he realized how truly dim the couple were. Instead, the doctor told the husband to go home and get a firecracker, light it, place it in a beer can, hold it to his ear and count to ten.

Figuring that both learned physicians couldn't be wrong, the redneck went home, lit a firecracker and put it in a beer can. He held the can up to his ear and began to count. '1, 2, 3, 4, 5…' At which point he paused, placed the beer can between his legs and resumed counting on his other hand.

A bartender leaned over to a guy sitting at the bar and said, 'Do you want to hear a redneck joke?'

The guy replied, 'Before you tell that joke, I think there's something you oughtta know: I'm six-foot tall, two hundred pounds and a redneck. The guy next to me is six-foot two, two hundred and thirty pounds and a redneck. And the guy next to him is six-foot four, two hundred and seventy pounds and a redneck. Now do you still want to tell that joke?'

'No,' said the bartender, 'not if I'm going to have to explain it three times.'

What's the difference between a good ole boy and a redneck?

– The good ole boy raises livestock, the redneck gets emotionally involved.

How does a redneck spell 'farm'?

– E I E I O.

What's the last thing you usually hear before a redneck dies?

– 'Hey, y'all, watch this!'

Did you hear about the redneck who passed away and left his entire estate in trust for his beloved widow?

– She can't touch it until she's fourteen.

🖤

Entering the town post office, a redneck spotted a new notice on the wall: MAN WANTED FOR ROBBERY IN WISCONSIN.

'Damn!' he said. 'If only that job was for Arkansas, I'd be goin' for it.'

RELIGION

Afraid that he would be late for an important business meeting in London, a motorist was beginning to panic because he couldn't find a parking space. Street after street was full and, becoming increasingly desperate, he decided to seek help from God.

Looking up to Heaven, he said, 'Lord, please help me out. If you find me a parking space, I'll give up drink and women and go to church every Sunday.'

Then as he turned the corner, miraculously a parking space appeared.

He looked skyward again and said, 'Never mind, I found one.'

A man went to confession and admitted that for years he had been stealing supplies from the timber yard where he worked.

'What did you take?' asked the priest.

'Enough to build my own house, a house for my son, houses for my two daughters, and a country cottage by the river.'

'This is a very serious matter,' said the priest. 'I shall have to think of a suitably severe penance. Tell me, have you ever done a retreat?'

'No, I haven't, Father,' said the man. 'But if you can get the plans, I can get the wood.'

A priest and several nuns lived in a quiet rural parish. One day, one of the older nuns noticed that the rugs in the church were beginning to fray. So she went to the priest and said, 'Father, I think your rugs need to be replaced soon.'

The priest thanked her for bringing it to his attention, and told her that he thought she had been there long enough to refer to church property as 'our' instead of 'your'.

Several days later, the same nun noticed that the

church hedge needed trimming. She again went to the priest and told him, 'Father, I've noticed that your... I mean, our, hedge needs to be trimmed.'

The priest thanked her for bringing the matter to his attention and also asked her whether she had seen his watch because it had gone missing. She said she hadn't, but assured him that she would look for it.

A few days later, the bishop paid a surprise visit to the parish. Just as he arrived, the same nun ran into church and called to the priest, 'Father, I've found your watch!'

'Bless you, my dear!' said the priest. 'Where did you find it?'

The nun replied, 'It was under our bed.'

A man was hit by a bus on a city street, and as he lay dying, a crowd gathered around him.

'Somebody fetch me a priest!' gasped the dying man. A policeman hurriedly checked the crowd, but there was no priest or any other man of God.

'A priest, please!' the dying man repeated.

Then out of the crowd stepped a little old man. 'Officer,' he said, 'I'm not a priest, I'm not even a Catholic, but for the past thirty-six years I have lived behind St Joseph's Catholic Church, and every night I overhear the Catholic litany. Perhaps I can be of some comfort to this poor man.'

The policeman thought it was a good idea and took the old man over to where the accident victim lay dying. The pensioner knelt down gingerly, leaned over the man and announced in a solemn voice, 'One little duck, number two; doctor's orders, number nine; two fat ladies, eighty-eight…'

Two nuns were riding their bicycles along the back streets of Rome.

One leaned over to the other and said, 'I've never come this way before.'

The other nun whispered, 'It must be the cobblestones.'

Having not attended church for many years, a man sought to atone for his sins by going to confession. He pulled aside the curtain on the confessional box, entered and sat down. He was amazed to find a fully equipped bar with crystal glasses, the best vestry wine, Guinness on tap, cigars and liqueur chocolates nearby, and on the wall a display of buxom young women in various states of undress.

He heard a priest come in. 'Forgive me, Father,' said the man, 'but it's been a long time since I last went to confession and I must admit the confessional box is a lot more inviting than it used to be.'

'Get out, you idiot,' said the priest. 'You're on my side.'

A man trying to understand the nature of God asked him, 'God, how long is a million years to you?'

God answered, 'A million years is like a minute.'

Then the man asked, 'God, how much is a million dollars to you?'

And God replied, 'A million dollars is like a penny.'

Finally, the man asked, 'God, could you give me a penny?'

And God said, 'In a minute.'

A young woman went to confession. She said, 'Bless me, Father, for I have sinned. Last night, my boyfriend made love to me six times.'

The priest said, 'You must go home and suck the juice of seven lemons.'

'And will that absolve me?' asked the young woman.

'No,' replied the priest, 'but it will take that smug look off your face.'

What's the difference between people who pray in church and people who pray in casinos?
 – The ones who pray in casinos are deadly serious.

Two nuns – Sister Mathematical (SM) and Sister Logical (SL) – were walking back to the convent late one night when they became aware of a man following them and getting ever closer.

SM: That man has been following us for the last sixteen and a half minutes. What do you think he wants?

SL: It's logical. He wants to attack us.

SM: Oh, no. At his current rate of progress he will reach us in four minutes and twelve seconds. What can we do?

SL: The only logical thing is for us to walk faster.

SM: It's not working.

SL: Of course it's not working. The man did the only logical thing. He started to walk faster, too.

SM: So what shall we do? At this rate, he'll reach us in

precisely two minutes but we're still over eight minutes from the convent.

SL: The only logical thing we can do is split up. You go that way and I'll go this way. He can't follow us both.

The man decided to follow Sister Logical, allowing Sister Mathematical to make it safely to the convent. Shortly afterwards, Sister Logical reached the convent, too.

SM: Sister Logical! Thank God, you made it! I was so worried about you. What happened after I left you?

SL: The only logical thing happened. The man couldn't follow us both, so he followed me.

SM: Yes, yes! But what happened then?

SL: The only logical thing happened. I started to run as fast as I could and he started to run as fast as he could.

SM: And?

SL: The only logical thing happened. He caught up with me.

SM: What did you do?

SL: The only logical thing to do. I lifted up my dress.

SM: Oh, Sister! What did the man do?

SL: The only logical thing to do. He pulled down his pants.

SM: Oh, no! What happened then?

SL: Isn't it logical, Sister? A nun with her dress up can run faster than a man with his pants down.

One Sunday, a cowboy went to church. When he entered, he saw that he and the preacher were the only ones present. The preacher asked the cowboy if he wanted him to go ahead and preach.

The cowboy said, 'I'm not too smart, but if I went to feed my cattle and only one showed up, I'd feed him.'

So the minister began his sermon. One hour passed, then two hours, then two and a half hours. The preacher finally finished and came down to ask the cowboy how he had liked the sermon.

The cowboy answered slowly, 'Well, I'm not very smart, but if I went to feed my cattle and only one showed up, I sure wouldn't feed him all the hay.'

George and Violet attended the same small-town church, where every week Violet taught Sunday school. After admiring her from afar for years, George finally plucked up the courage to ask Violet out to dinner. To his delight, she accepted and he booked them a table at his favourite restaurant.

At the restaurant, he asked her, 'Would you like some wine with dinner?'

'Oh, no, George,' said Violet. 'What would I tell my Sunday school class?'

George was shaken by her reaction and didn't say much more until the end of the meal when he pulled out a packet of cigarettes and said, 'Would you like a cigarette, Violet?'

'Oh, no, George,' said Violet. 'What would I tell my Sunday school class?'

By now, George was feeling thoroughly disillusioned. He drove Violet home in virtual silence but on the way they passed a motel. Reasoning that he had nothing to lose after two setbacks, he asked her if she wanted to spend the night at the motel with him.

'That would be nice, George,' she said.

George was astonished by her response and quickly checked them both in to the motel, where they enjoyed a night of raw passion.

The next morning, he asked her, 'What are you going to tell your Sunday school class?'

Violet replied, 'The same as I always tell them: you don't have to drink or smoke to have a good time.'

A deacon at the Assembly of God, who as well as being a devout Christian was also a proud veteran of the United

States Marine Corps, was being bothered by one of those religious groups that go door-to-door in the community. This particular group had called on him unannounced on several occasions and he had become so irritated by their visits that he went to his pastor and said, "How can I get rid of these people?"

The pastor said, 'I know what these people are like. They don't believe in saluting the flag. They don't believe in singing the National Anthem. So the next time they come, you just make them pledge allegiance to the flag and sing the National Anthem, and after that they'll go away and leave you alone.'

So the deacon went out and bought the biggest US flag he could find and put it on the wall of his home. He found a copy of the National Anthem and taught his family every verse. He thought to himself, 'I will be ready for them next time they call.'

One morning, he looked out and saw a woman smartly dressed in dark clothes and carrying a satchel. As she walked slowly up to his door, he thought, 'I'm going to teach you a lesson once and for all.' Before she could even knock on the door, he opened it, grabbed her by the arm, brought her inside and said, 'Stand right there! I want you to do something before you say a word or open your mouth in my home. First of all, we are going to pledge allegiance to the flag.'

So together, the deacon, his family and the lady visitor pledged allegiance to the flag of the United States of America. Then, he said to her, 'Now, you are going to sing the National Anthem with my family, and we're going to sing all the verses.' They sang all the verses to the National Anthem, and the visitor sang right along with them.

At the end, he said proudly, 'Now, lady, how do you like that?'

She said, 'I think it's wonderful, and I'll be honest with you, I've been selling Avon for twenty-three years and I've never before had a welcome like this!'

A small boy got on a bus and found himself sitting opposite a priest. Intrigued, the boy asked him why he wore his collar that way.

The priest answered, 'Because I am a Father.'

The boy said, 'My dad doesn't wear his collar like that.'

'Yes,' said the priest, 'but I am the Father of many.'

The boy said, 'My dad has three boys and two girls, but he doesn't wear his collar that way.'

The priest, becoming impatient, explained, 'I am the Father of hundreds.'

'In that case,' said the boy, 'maybe you should wear your pants backwards instead of your collar.'

Did you hear about the Dial-a-Prayer service for atheists?
 - You call up, it rings and rings, but nobody answers.

A ninety-two-year-old Mother Superior was dying at a convent in Ireland, and all the nuns gathered around her bed in an attempt to make her last journey comfortable. They offered her some warm milk to drink but she refused. Then one of the nuns took the glass back to the kitchen. Remembering a bottle of Irish whiskey received as a gift the previous Christmas, she opened and poured a generous amount into the warm milk.

Back at the Mother Superior's bed, she held the glass to her lips. The Mother Superior drank a little, then a little more and before they knew it, she had drunk the whole glass down to the last drop.

'Mother Superior,' the nuns asked solemnly, 'is there a piece of wisdom and advice that you can impart to us before you die?'

With a weak smile, she turned to them and said, 'Don't sell that cow.'

One Sunday, a pastor told his congregation that the church needed some extra money, and he asked the people to consider donating a little more than usual into the offering plate. He said that whoever gave the most would be able to pick out three hymns. After the offering plates were passed around, the pastor glanced down and noticed that someone had given a one-thousand-dollar bill. He was so excited that he immediately shared his joy with his congregation and said he'd like to thank the person who placed the money in the plate.

An elderly lady shyly raised her hand at the back of the church. The pastor asked her to come to the front and she did so. He told her how wonderful it was that she gave so much, and in thanks asked her to pick out three hymns. Her eyes brightened as she looked over the congregation, pointed to the three most handsome men in the building and said, 'I'll take him and him and him.'

A preacher was concluding his temperance sermon with a passionate tirade. 'If I had all the beer in the world,' he roared, 'I'd take it and throw it into the river.'

And the congregation cried, 'Amen!'

'If I had all the wine in the world,' bellowed the preacher, 'I'd take it and throw it in the river.'

And the congregation cried, 'Amen!'

'If I had all the whisky and rum in the world,' barked the preacher, 'I'd take it and throw it in the river.'

And the congregation cried, 'Hallelujah!'

With that, the preacher sat down. The song leader then stood up nervously and announced, 'For our closing song, let us sing hymn number 240, "Shall We Gather At The River..."'

An elderly vicar was talking to one of his parishioners. He said, 'When you reach my age, you spend a lot more time thinking about the hereafter.'

'Why do you say that?' asked the parishioner.

The vicar replied, 'Well, I often find myself going into a room and thinking, "What did I come in here after?"'

A priest, a minister and a rabbi were playing poker in the back room of a bar when the police raided the game. Addressing the priest, the police officer in charge said, 'Father Kelly, were you gambling?'

Turning his eyes to Heaven, the priest whispered, 'Lord, forgive me for what I am about to do.' And then he told the policeman firmly, 'No, officer, I was not gambling.'

The officer then asked the minister, 'Pastor Richards, were you gambling?'

The minister whispered an apology to God before answering, 'No, officer, I was not gambling.'

Turning finally to the rabbi, the officer asked, 'Rabbi Rosenthal, were you gambling?'

Shrugging his shoulders, the rabbi replied, 'With whom?'

Jesus, Joseph and Mary were doing chores around their home in Nazareth when Jesus suddenly ran outside to Joseph and asked, 'Did you call me?'

'No, I'm sorry,' Joseph replied. 'I just hit my thumb with the hammer again.'

Two nuns were walking through the park when they were attacked by two thugs. Their habits were ripped from them, and the men began sexually assaulting them.

One nun cast her eyes heavenward and cried, 'Forgive him, Lord, for he knows not what he is doing!'

The other nun turned to her and said, 'Mine does!'

A man was driving along the road when his car broke down near a monastery. He knocked on the monastery door and asked if he could stay the night.

The monks graciously accepted him, fed him dinner and even fixed his car. Later, as the man tried to fall asleep, he heard a strange sound – a sound like no other he had ever heard. The next morning, he asked the monks what the sound was, but they said, 'We can't tell you because you're not a monk.'

The man was disappointed but thanked them for their hospitality and resumed his journey. As fate would have it, two years later his car broke down outside the same monastery. Again the monks accepted him, fed him and repaired his car. That night, he heard the same weird sound that he had heard before. The next morning, he asked the monks what the sound was, but they said, 'We can't tell you because you're not a monk.'

The man said, 'My curiosity is killing me. I have to know what that sound is. If you can't tell me because I'm not a monk, then how do I go about becoming a monk?'

The monks said, 'You must travel the world and tell us how many trees there are. When you find the number, you will become a monk.'

So the man set off around the world counting every tree. Forty years later, he returned to the monastery and announced, 'I have completed the task you set me. There are 200,459,312,648,332 trees in the world.'

'Congratulations!' said the monks. 'You are now officially a monk. Therefore, we can reveal the truth about the sound.'

They led him to a wooden door, and the head monk said, 'The sound is behind that door.'

The head monk turned the handle but the door was locked, so he asked for the key. The other monks gave him the key and he opened the door. Behind the wooden door was another door made of stone. The head monk requested the key to the stone door. The other monks gave him the key and he opened it, only to find a door made of ruby. He demanded another key from the monks, who provided it. Behind that was another door made of sapphire, and so it went on until the man and the monks had gone through doors made of emerald, topaz, amethyst and silver. Before them now stood a door made of gold.

'This is the last door,' said the head monk. 'Behind that is the sound.'

The man was so relieved that he would finally solve the mystery of the sound. With feverish anticipation, he unlocked the gold door, turned the handle, opened the door and was astonished to find the source of that strange sound. It was a truly unbelievable sight.

But I can't tell you what it was because you're not a monk.

RESTAURANTS

A man was sitting in a restaurant when he suddenly felt the need to break wind. Since the music was really loud, he decided to time his gas to the beat of the music. After a couple of songs, he started to feel a lot better but as he finished his coffee he noticed that everybody was staring at him. That was when he remembered that he was listening to his iPod.

A resident in a five-star hotel was ordering breakfast in the establishment's Palm Court restaurant. He told the waiter, 'I'd like one under-cooked egg so that it's runny, and one over-cooked egg so that it's tough and hard to eat. I'd also like two cold rashers of grilled bacon, sausages that are black on one side and pink on the other, some burned toast, butter straight from the freezer so that it's impossible to spread, and a pot of very weak, lukewarm coffee.'

'That's quite a complicated order,' said the waiter, nonplussed. 'It might be difficult.'

'It shouldn't be that difficult,' said the man sarcastically, 'because that's exactly what you brought me yesterday.'

A man went into a restaurant and ordered a bowl of chilli. 'Sorry,' said the waiter, 'the lady on the next table had the last one.'

The man looked across to the next table and noticed that although the woman had clearly finished her meal, the bowl of chilli was still half full. He called over, 'Are you going to eat that?'

'No,' she replied. 'You can have it.'

The man eagerly tucked into the remains of the chilli but after a few mouthfuls he saw a dead mouse in it and threw up into the bowl.

'Yes,' said the woman. 'That was as far as I got, too.'

A man and his wife walked into an expensive restaurant and asked for a table.

'I'm sorry, sir,' said the maître d', 'but there are no tables available tonight.'

'Huh!' said the man. 'I bet if the President of the United States were to walk in now and ask for a table, there would be one available.'

'Well, yes,' replied the maître d', 'I expect there would.'

'Then I'll take that table,' said the man, 'because the President isn't coming.'

Did you hear about the restaurant that serves chicken dinners for a dollar?
- You sit down and the waiter brings you a plate of bird seed.

When the waitress came to take his order, the middle-aged man said, 'I want a quickie.'

The waitress slapped his face.

Shortly afterwards another waitress passed and the

man said, 'I want a quickie.'

She, too, slapped his face.

Then another waitress appeared and the man said, 'Please, can I have a quickie?'

Again the man got his face slapped. At that point a diner at the next table leaned over and said, 'I think you'll find it's pronounced "keesh".'

If white wine goes with fish, do white grapes go with sushi?

After eating a sumptuous steak in a city centre restaurant, Peter was so impressed that he told all his friends about the place. So the next day, Peter returned to the restaurant with five friends. They were shown to a table at the back of the restaurant and ordered their steaks. However, when the waiter brought their order, the steaks were tiny.

An embarrassed Peter berated the waiter. 'When I was here yesterday, you served me a lovely big juicy steak – the largest steak I've ever had. But today's steaks are pathetic, shrivelled specimens. What's going on? Why are they so different?'

'Ah, yes,' said the waiter. 'You see, yesterday you were sitting by the window…'

A man in a fish restaurant had waited forty-five minutes for his meal. Eventually, the waiter, sensing the customer's growing impatience, came over and said, 'I do apologize, sir. Your fish will be with you very shortly.'

'Very well,' said the customer, 'but if you don't mind my asking: what sort of bait are you using?'

A customer was bothering the waiter in a restaurant. First, he asked for the air conditioning to be turned up because he was too hot, then he asked for it to be turned down because he was too cold. This went on for about half an hour, but although the waiter kept rushing back and forth he remained surprisingly patient.

Finally, a second customer asked him, 'Why don't you just tell that pest to leave?'

'I really don't mind,' smiled the waiter. 'We don't even have an air conditioner.'

What happened when the lights were too bright at a Chinese restaurant?

  - The manager decided to dim sum.

An American tourist went into a restaurant in Barcelona and noticed a dish called 'cojones' on the menu. So he asked the waiter, 'What are cojones?'

The waiter explained, 'They are the testicles of a fighting bull that has died in the ring.'

The tourist decided to be adventurous and ordered them, and they were so delicious that he returned to the restaurant the following evening and ordered cojones again. But this time instead of the huge juicy testicles he enjoyed on his first visit, he was given shrivelled specimens that were no bigger than walnuts.

He summoned the waiter. 'What's happened to the cojones?' he demanded. 'These are half the size of last night's. What sort of bull had these?'

'Remember, sir,' said the waiter, 'the bull does not always lose...'

An explorer was staggering through the desert, desperate for water, when he spotted something far off in the distance. Hoping to find water, he walked towards the image but when he got there he found it was just an old man sitting at a card table with a bunch of neckties laid out on it.

'Water! Water! I need water,' the explorer gasped.

'Sorry,' said the old man, 'I don't have any water, but why don't you buy a nice tie? Here's one that will go well with your shirt.'

'I don't want to buy a tie, you idiot!' the explorer shouted. 'I need water.'

'OK, don't buy a tie then,' said the old man. 'There's no need to lose your temper. Since I'm a kindly soul, I'll tell you that if you head over that big sand dune and keep walking for five miles, you'll find a restaurant that my brother runs. You'll get all the water you need there.'

The explorer thanked him and set off over the big dune before eventually disappearing from view. Three hours later, he came crawling back to where the old man was sitting at his card table.

The old man said, 'I told you, my brother's restaurant is about five miles over that big sand dune. Couldn't you find it?'

'I found it,' the explorer gasped. 'But they wouldn't let me in without a tie.'

SCHOOL AND COLLEGE

One day while walking along the street, a man bumped into his old schoolteacher. The man told him, 'You were right when you said I wouldn't amount to anything.'

'Ha! I knew you'd end up on the dole!'

'I'm not on the dole,' said the man. 'I'm a teacher.'

An inflatable boy went to an inflatable school where he was having a really bad day. Bored with the English lesson, he walked out of the inflatable classroom but then saw the inflatable headmaster approaching him.

The inflatable boy pulled out a pin and punctured the inflatable headmaster before running out of the inflatable school gates. Just as he got past the gates, he thought about how much he hated school and once more pulled out his pin and poked it into the inflatable school. He then ran as fast as his inflatable legs allowed, all the way home to his inflatable bedroom.

A couple of hours later, the inflatable police turned up at his house. Panicking, the inflatable boy pulled out the pin and jabbed it into himself. He woke up in an inflatable hospital and, in the bed next to him, he saw the inflatable headmaster.

Shaking his deflated head, more in sorrow than in anger, the headmaster said, 'You've let me down, you've let the school down, but worst of all, you've let yourself down.'

Teacher: That's quite a cough you have. What are you taking for it?
Little Johnny: I don't know, miss. What will you give me?

The teacher asked Little Johnny, 'Why weren't you at school yesterday?'

Johnny replied, 'My grandpa got burned.'

'I'm sorry to hear that,' said the teacher. 'He wasn't burned too badly, was he?'

'Oh, yes,' said Johnny. 'They really know what they're doing at those crematoriums.'

One boy at school always claimed that the dog had eaten his homework. Nobody believed him until the dog graduated from Harvard.

A new teacher was trying to make use of her psychology training. She started her class by saying, 'Everyone who thinks they are stupid, stand up.'

After a few seconds, one of her students stood up.

'So,' she asked him. 'Do you think you are stupid?'

'No, ma'am,' replied the student, 'but I hate to see you standing there all by yourself.'

School Answering Machine

You have reached the automated answering service of your child's school. In order to assist you in connecting to the right staff member, please listen to all options before making a selection.

To lie about why your child is absent, press 1.

To make excuses for why your child did not do his/her homework, press 2.

To complain about what we do, press 3.

To abuse our staff members verbally, press 4.

To request another teacher for the third time this year, press 5.

To complain about bus transportation, press 6.

To complain about school lunches, press 7.

To complain about why your child was not given the lead role in the school play, press 8.

To tell us that your child is innocent and that it was all Hannah McGrath's fault, press 9.

If you want us to raise your child, press 0.

Teacher: On Monday you said your homework blew away. On Tuesday you said your father accidentally took it to work with him. On Wednesday you said your little sister tore it up. On Thursday you said someone

stole it. Today I asked you to bring your parents to school. Now, where are they?
Little Johnny: The dog ate them.

Teacher: Where's your homework assignment?
Little Johnny: It blew away while I was on my way to school.
Teacher: And why were you so late for school this morning?
Little Johnny: I had to wait for a strong wind.

Little Johnny: I'm tired of doing homework.
Father: Now, son, hard work never killed anyone.
Little Johnny: I know, but I don't want to be the first.

Teacher: If there are eight flies on my desk and I hit one with a ruler, how many are left?
Little Johnny: The squashed one.

Mary: Our teacher talks to herself. Does yours?
Johnny: Yes, but she doesn't realize it. She thinks we're actually listening.

The teacher at an English primary school stood in front of a map of the world.

'Josh,' she said, 'can you show me where on this map America is?'

Josh pointed correctly to America.

'Now, Chloe,' continued the teacher, 'can you tell me the name of the person who discovered America?'

Chloe replied, 'Josh just did, miss.'

A Student's Letter Home
'It's been three months since coming to college. I am sorry for my thoughtlessness not writing until now. I'll bring you up to date, but before you read on, please sit down. DON'T READ ANY FURTHER UNLESS YOU ARE SITTING DOWN. OK! Things are getting better. My skull fracture and concussion are almost healed. They happened as I jumped out of my dormitory window during the fire. I'm down to only one sick headache per day. I was so lucky that gas station attendant, working near the dorm, saw both the fire and my jump. He called the fire department and the ambulance. He also visited me at the hospital. Since I had nowhere to live because the dormitory burned, he invited me to share his apartment with him. It's really

just a basement room but it's kind of cute. He's a very fine boy. We're deeply in love and are getting married. We haven't set the exact date yet but it will be before I start to show. Yes, I'm pregnant. I know how much you're looking forward to being grandparents and I know you will welcome the baby and give it the same devotion and tender loving care you gave me as a baby. We have to delay our wedding because my boyfriend's minor infection prevents us from passing our pre-marital blood tests. Stupid me! I caught it from him. It will clear up with the daily penicillin injections. I know you'll welcome him into our family with open arms. He's not educated but he's kind. He's ambitious and although he's of a different race and religion than ours, I'm sure you will love him as I do. His family background is strong. His father is an important gun-bearer in his native village. Now that I have brought you up to date. I confess there was no dormitory fire. I didn't have a concussion or a skull fracture. I wasn't in hospital. I am not pregnant. I don't have VD and there's no man in my life. I am, however, getting a 'D' in History and an 'F' in Science. I just wanted you to see those marks in the proper perspective.'

SEX

A man was having problems getting aroused for sex, so he went to see a doctor. The doctor told him, 'To be perfectly frank, your equipment is worn out. You have used it too often. I would say that you can probably only have sex twenty more times for the rest of your life.'

Deeply depressed, the man went home and told his wife what the doctor had said. 'Oh, no!' she cried. 'Only twenty more times! We shouldn't waste them, darling; we should make a list.'

'I already made a list on the way home,' he said. 'Sorry, your name's not on it.'

A married couple had agreed to take part in a blood donor scheme, and as part of the pre-screening process, a female volunteer visited their home to ask them a series of personal questions.

The volunteer asked the husband, 'Have you ever paid for sex?'

Glancing wearily over at his wife who was trying to calm a new baby as well as tend to several other children milling around her, he sighed, 'Every time!'

A husband arrived home early from work and heard strange noises coming from the bedroom. He rushed upstairs to find his wife naked on the bed, sweating and panting.

'What's up?' he cried.

'I'm having a heart attack,' she gasped.

He ran downstairs to phone for an ambulance, but as he did so his young son said, 'Daddy! Daddy! Uncle Pete's hiding in your wardrobe and he's got no clothes on!'

The husband immediately rushed back upstairs into the bedroom, past his screaming wife, and ripped open the wardrobe door to reveal his brother, totally naked, cowering in the corner.

'I don't believe it!' he yelled. 'My wife's having a heart attack and you're running around with no clothes on scaring the kids!'

A couple with hectic lifestyles decided they needed to use a code to indicate that they wanted to have sex without letting their young children know. The word they settled on was 'typewriter'.

One day, the father said to his four-year-old daughter, 'Go tell Mommy that Daddy needs to type a letter.'

The child told her mother what he had said and the mother responded, 'Go tell Daddy that he can't type a letter right now because there's a red ribbon in the typewriter.'

The child relayed the information to her father.

A few days later, the mother told the daughter, 'Go tell Daddy that he can type that letter now.'

The child delivered the message to her father but returned to her mother and announced, 'Daddy said never mind with the typewriter, he already wrote the letter by hand.'

What do you call kinky sex with chocolate?
 - S&M&M.

A young man bumped into a friend at the bar. 'How are you doing?' he asked.

'I was great… until last night.'

'Why? What happened last night?'

'My girlfriend and I were talking about how many people we had slept with.'

'Oh. What did she say?'

'She said she could count the number of guys she's slept with on one hand.'

'That's good, surely?'

"Yes, that's what I thought. But then I saw that she was holding a calculator.'

A honeymoon couple went into a hotel and asked for a suite. 'Bridal?' asked the desk clerk.

'No, it's OK,' said the bride. 'I'll just hang on to his shoulders.'

Frank was one of life's great optimists. He always looked on the bright side even though his friends found it infuriating. No matter what the situation, Frank's response was always: 'It could have been worse.'

In an attempt to cure him of his irritating habit, his friends decided to invent a situation so bleak and terrible that not even Frank could find a reason for optimism. So in their favourite bar, one of them said: 'Frank, did you hear about Mike? He came home last night, found his wife in bed with another man, shot them both and then turned the gun on himself!'

'That's awful,' said Frank, 'but it could have been worse.'

'How the hell could it possibly have been worse?' asked his friends incredulously.

'Well,' replied Frank, 'if it had happened the night before, I'd be dead now.'

A middle-aged man and woman met, fell in love and decided to get married. Settling into the bridal suite at their hotel on their wedding night, the bride turned to her groom and said, 'Please promise to be gentle. I am still a virgin.'

The startled groom replied, 'How can that be? You've been married three times!'

The bride replied, 'Well, you see, my first husband was a psychiatrist and all he ever wanted to do was talk about it. My second husband was an astronomer and all he ever wanted to do was look at it.' Catching her breath, she added, 'And my third husband was a stamp collector and all he ever wanted to do was... Oh, God, I miss him!'

Why Chocolate is Better Than Sex

• Chocolate satisfies even when it has gone soft.

• You can make chocolate last as long as you want it to.

• You can have chocolate even in front of your mother.

• Chocolate doesn't get you pregnant.

• When you have chocolate it doesn't keep your neighbours awake.

• You don't need to fake your enjoyment of chocolate.

• Good chocolate is easy to find.

• You can have chocolate at any time of the month.

• You can ask a stranger for chocolate without getting your face slapped.

What's a man's idea of safe sex?
- A padded headboard.

What's a man's idea of foreplay?
- Half an hour of begging.

A little boy hid in his parents' bedroom closet because he wanted to see what took place in their room when the doors were locked. As he peeked through the slats of the closet door, he saw his mother and her boyfriend having sex. Suddenly the boy's father came home and the wife quickly shoved her boyfriend into the closet – the same closet her son was in.

After a minute or so, the boy said to the man, 'Gee, it's dark in here.'

Shocked to find that he was not alone, the man just nodded his head in agreement.

A few minutes later, the boy said, 'Wanna buy my baseball glove?'

To ease his guilt, the man asked, 'How much?'

The boy replied, 'Fifty dollars.'

The man said, 'OK.'

Ten minutes later, the boy asked the man if he'd like to buy his baseball bat for fifty dollars as well. The man reluctantly agreed.

Eventually, the boy's father left the house, and his mother dragged her boyfriend from the closet before sending him on his way.

The next morning at the breakfast table, the little boy pulled out a roll of money and began counting it. His mother asked, 'Where did that come from?'

'I can't say,' said the boy, and when he repeatedly refused to give an answer, she told him to get in the car. She then drove him to church, where she ordered him to get into the confessional and tell the priest where he got the money. As the priest slid the confessional door across, the boy said, 'Gee, it's dark in here.'

The priest said, 'Don't start all that again!'

A Frenchman and an Italian were seated next to a Norwegian on an overseas flight. After a few drinks, the men began discussing their love lives. 'Last night, I made love to my wife four times,' the Frenchman bragged, 'and this morning, she made me delicious crêpes and she told me how much she adored me.'

'Ah, last night, I made love to my wife six times,' the Italian responded, 'and this morning, she made me a wonderful cappuccino and told me she could never love another man.'

When the Norwegian remained silent, the Frenchman asked smugly, 'And how many times did you make love to your wife last night?'

'Once,' he replied.

'Only once?' the Italian snorted. 'And what did she say to you this morning?'

'Don't stop.'

A husband arrived home to find his wife naked in bed with another man.

'What are you doing?' cried the husband.

The wife turned to her lover and said, 'See, I told you he was stupid.'

Three couples – an elderly couple, a middle-aged couple and a young newlywed couple – wanted to join a church. The pastor said, 'We have special conditions for new parishioners. In order to be accepted, you must abstain from having sex for two weeks.'

The couples agreed to the terms and returned two weeks later.

The pastor asked the elderly couple, 'Were you able to

abstain from having sex for two weeks?'

'No problem at all,' said the old man.

'Congratulations! Welcome to our church,' said the pastor.

Then the pastor asked the middle-aged couple, 'Were you able to abstain from sex for two weeks?'

The husband replied, 'It was difficult at times, particularly during the second week, but we made it.'

'Congratulations! Welcome to our church,' said the pastor.

Finally, the pastor asked the young newlyweds, 'Were you able to abstain from having sex for two weeks?'

'No, pastor,' replied the young man sadly.

'What happened?' asked the pastor.

The young man said, 'Halfway through the second week, my wife went to lift a packet of frozen peas out of the freezer and dropped it. When she bent down to pick it up, I was overcome with lust and took advantage of her right there.'

'I'm sorry,' said the pastor, 'but you realize this means you will not be welcome in our church?'

'We know,' said the young man. 'We're not welcome at the supermarket any more either.'

SHOPPING

A middle-aged man walked into a shoe shop and asked for a pair of shoes, size eight.

The sales assistant said, 'Are you sure, sir? You look like a size twelve to me.'

'Just bring me a size eight,' insisted the customer.

So the assistant fetched a pair of size eight shoes, and the man squeezed his feet into them with obvious discomfort. He then stood up in the shoes, but with considerable pain.

'Are you absolutely sure you want these shoes?' repeated the assistant.

'Listen,' said the man. 'My wife's been having an affair,

I can barely afford the mortgage on my house, I work for a tyrant, my daughter's going out with a junkie and my son has just announced that he's gay. The only pleasure I have left in life is to come home at night and take my shoes off!'

A man went into a hardware store and asked for a chainsaw that could cut down six trees in an hour. The sales assistant recommended a top-of-the-range model, and the man was so impressed by the description that he bought it.

The next day, however, he returned to the store in a foul mood. 'That chainsaw you sold me is useless,' he raged. 'It took me all day to cut down just one tree!'

The sales assistant took the chainsaw and started it up to see what the problem was.

The man said, 'What's that noise?'

Arriving at the office one morning, seventy-five-year-old Clive was reminded by his secretary that it was his wife's birthday. That lunchtime he went shopping but he couldn't think of anything to buy her until he passed a lingerie store and realized that in all their years of marriage he had never before bought her any underwear. Going inside, he saw an expensive, beautiful negligee and decided to buy it to make his wife feel young and sexy again. He told the sales assistant to wrap it and then he rushed home to see his wife.

He found her in the kitchen, handed her the gift and told her to go upstairs and unwrap it while he waited downstairs.

Opening the package, she saw a negligee so sheer it left nothing to the imagination. She thought it was a lovely gesture, but decided to give her husband an even bigger thrill by going downstairs stark naked.

Leaving the negligee on the bed, she took off all her clothes and set off downstairs. 'Clive, come and see,' she called out.

Clive walked into the hallway, looked up at his wife and exclaimed, 'All that money I paid and they didn't even iron it!'

A woman was telling her neighbour about the new local supermarket. 'It's very state-of-the-art and designed to make shopping a natural and relaxing experience. It has an automatic water mister to keep all the fruit fresh. Just before it switches on, you hear the sound of distant thunder and smell the aroma of fresh rain. As you approach the milk aisle, you hear cows mooing and there's the scent of fresh hay. As you approach the eggs, you hear hens clucking and the air is filled with the delicious smell of bacon and eggs frying. And the vegetable department features the aroma of fresh buttered corn.'

'It sounds wonderful,' enthused the neighbour.

'Yes, but I don't buy toilet paper there any more.'

A woman went into a furniture store, chose a table lamp she liked and took it to the sales desk.

'That's $79.95,' said the store owner.

'But this same lamp is only $59.95 at the store down the street,' she protested.

'Then, why don't you buy it there?'

'Because they've sold out.'

'Ah,' smiled the store owner, 'when I've sold out of them, they're only $49.95.'

A young man wanted to buy a birthday present for his

girlfriend, and took along her sister to the department store for advice. He eventually decided to buy his sweetheart a pair of white gloves, and the sister bought a pair of panties for herself. However, while wrapping the items, the sales assistant accidentally mixed them up so that the sister got the gloves and the young man got the panties. Without checking the contents of the package, the young man mailed it to his girlfriend along with this note:

'My dearest Hermione, I chose these because I noticed you are not in the habit of wearing any when we go out in the evening. If it had not been for your sister, I would have chosen the long ones with buttons, but she wears short ones that are easy to remove. These are a delicate shade but the lady I bought them from showed me the pair she had been wearing for the last three weeks and they were hardly soiled. I asked her to try yours on for me, and they looked really smart. I wish I was there to put them on you for the first time as no doubt other hands will come in contact with them before I have a chance to see you again. When you take them off, remember to blow in them before putting them away as they will naturally be a little damp from wearing. Just think how many times I will kiss them during the coming year. I hope you will wear them for me on Friday night. All my love, Charles.

'P.S. The latest style is to wear them folded down with a little fur showing.'

A woman called in to a furniture store and bought a self-assembly wardrobe for her bedroom. She took it home and painstakingly put it together. She was very pleased with her efforts until a train passed by close to her house and caused the wardrobe to collapse. Thinking it was a freak accident, she re-assembled the wardrobe but once again it collapsed when the next train rattled past.

So she went back to the store to complain, and the store sent out a repair man to investigate the problem. He arrived just in time to see the wardrobe collapse once more as a train passed by. Puzzled by the malfunction, he decided to rebuild the wardrobe and sit inside it to see if he could stop it from collapsing.

Seconds after the repair man climbed inside, the woman's husband arrived home early from work. Seeing the wardrobe door half open, he peered in and saw the repair man crouching inside.

'Who the hell are you, and what are you doing in my bedroom?' he raged.

The repair man replied meekly, 'You're probably not going to believe this, but I'm waiting for a train.'

On a shopping expedition with her daughter, a mother spotted a luxurious fur coat in a store window. As she debated whether or not to buy it, her daughter warned, 'Remember, some poor, helpless creature has to suffer so you can have this.'

'Don't worry, honey,' said the mother. 'Your father won't get the bill for a couple of weeks yet.'

A new department store announced that it was going to give out free TVs to the first hundred people who came to the store on its Grand Opening Day. The store was scheduled to open at 9 a.m., but people were already camped out in front of the store by 6 a.m., determined to receive their free TV.

Shortly before 9 a.m., a little old man walked up to the front of the line and casually stepped in front of the man at the head of the queue – a big, burly guy who had been there for three hours. The big guy wasn't about to let this old guy cut in front of him, so he pushed the old man out of the way, sending him reeling to the ground. The little old man got up, dusted himself down and elbowed his way in front of the big burly man a second time. Once again, he was pushed away by the big man, this time even more forcefully than before. Yet again he got up, dusted himself down and stepped between the big, burly man and the door a third time!

This kept happening until finally a policeman heard the noise and rushed over to hear what the fight was about. 'Well,' said the big burly man, 'I've been here at the front of the line since early this morning, and this old man had the nerve to push in front of me.'

When asked to tell his side of the story, the little old man replied, 'What that man said is correct. I did push in front of him several times, and if he keeps shoving me away, I'm not going to open the store!'

Shopping in the fruit and vegetable section of a supermarket, a man asked a young member of staff if he could buy half a head of lettuce. The young man pointed out that the supermarket only sold whole lettuce heads but the customer was adamant and demanded that the store manager be consulted.

Walking into the back room, the young man said to the manager, 'Some asshole wants to buy half a head of lettuce.' As he finished the sentence, he turned to find the customer standing right behind him, so he added quickly, 'And this gentleman kindly offered to buy the other half.'

The manager approved the sale and the customer went on his way.

Later that day, the manager sought out the young

man and told him, 'I was impressed with the way you got yourself out of a potentially sticky situation earlier. In this company we like people who think on their feet. Where are you from, son?'

'Canada, sir,' the young man replied.

'Why did you leave Canada?'

'Well, sir,' said the young man, 'there's nothing but whores and hockey players up there.'

'Really!' The manager frowned. 'My wife is from Canada.'

'No kidding!' said the young man. 'Which team did she play for?'

A man went into a clothing store to buy a suit. The salesman asked him his name, age, religion, occupation, college, high school, hobbies, political party and his wife's maiden name.

'Why all the questions?' the customer asked. 'All I want is a suit.'

'Sir, this is not just an ordinary tailor's shop,' the salesman said. 'We don't merely sell you a suit. We find a suit that is exactly right for you. We make a study of your personality and your background and your surroundings. For the wool we send to the region of

Australia that has the kind of sheep to match your character. We then ship the wool to be woven in the precise area of Scotland where the climate is most sympathetic to your temperament. Then we fit and measure you carefully. Finally, after much careful thought and study, the suit is made. There are more fittings and more changes. And then...'

'Wait a minute,' said the customer. 'I need this suit tomorrow afternoon for my nephew's wedding!'

'Don't worry,' said the salesman. 'You'll have it.'

On a trip to a shopping mall, a couple agreed to split up, visit their favourite shops and meet up again an hour and a half later. So while he visited the camera shop and the sports shop, she homed in on the big ladies' fashion store. When he met up with her ninety minutes later outside the fashion store, she was carrying a dozen bags filled with clothes.

'I don't believe it!' he exclaimed. 'Have you really bought all that?'

'Well, yes,' she replied. Then gesturing towards the interior of the shop, she added, 'But look at all the stuff I'm leaving behind.'

SHOW BUSINESS

A man was hired by a circus to perform the most menial, unpleasant job of all – shovelling up the elephants' droppings as they walked around the ring. At the end of a particularly difficult shift, he met with his co-workers and complained about his lot in life.

'It's a horrible job,' he said. 'All I do night after night is shuffle around behind the ruddy elephants, dodging their piles of poop and then scooping it up into a bucket. It's filthy, smelly work. My arms are aching, my shoes are a mess and my clothes all stink of elephant dung.'

His colleagues agreed. 'Why don't you quit your job,' they suggested, 'and find something more rewarding?

You know you can do better than this place.'

'I know you're right,' he said, 'but I just can't give up the glamour of show business.'

Rihanna, Cher and Madonna have had a big falling-out. Apparently, they're no longer on first-name terms.

After spending most of the day drinking, two sailors on shore leave decided to go and see a variety show in the evening. During the interval, one of them needed to use the toilet and asked the usherette for directions.

She said, 'You go through the right-hand exit door, then turn left, then right, then along the corridor, turn right again and it's on your left.'

He followed the directions with considerable difficulty, relieved himself and eventually returned to his seat.

'You missed the best act,' said his friend. 'While you were gone, a sailor came on stage and pissed into the orchestra pit.'

A man said to his friend, 'My wife does amazing impressions of farm animals.'

'What's so good about them?' asked the friend.

'Well, she not only does the sounds, she does the smells, too.'

A Hollywood movie producer was lying next to the pool at the Beverly Hills Hilton when his business partner arrived. 'How did the meeting go?' asked the producer excitedly.

'Fantastic!' said the partner. 'Spielberg will direct for nine million, Clooney will star in it for twelve million and we can bring the whole picture in for under sixty million.'

'That calls for a celebration!' said the producer.

'There's just one catch,' the partner warned.

'What's that?'

'We have to put up two thousand in cash.'

A hypnotist called thirty people from the audience on stage and put them into a trance. He said, 'Whatever word I say, you will obey that command.'

The hypnotist said, 'Laugh.' And the thirty people instantly started laughing.

Then the hypnotist said, 'Moo.' And the thirty people instinctively started mooing.

Just then the hypnotist tripped over one of his props. 'Sh*t!' he exclaimed.

It took four hours to clean up the stage.

An out-of-work actor received a call from his agent one day. 'I've got you a job,' said the agent.

'That's great,' said the actor. 'What is it?'

'Well,' said the agent, 'it's a one-liner.'

'That's OK,' replied the actor. 'I've been out of work for so long I'll take anything. What's the line?'

The agent said, 'Hark, I hear the cannons roar.'

'I love it!' said the actor. 'When's the audition?'

'Wednesday,' replied the agent. Wednesday came and the actor arrived at the audition. He marched on stage and shouted, 'Hark, I hear the cannons roar!'

'Brilliant!' said the director. 'You've got the job. Be here nine o'clock Saturday evening.'

The actor was so excited about finally getting a job that he went out and got horribly drunk. He woke up at 8.30 on Saturday evening and ran to the theatre, continually repeating his line, 'Hark, I hear the cannons roar! Hark, I hear the cannons roar! Hark, I hear the cannons roar!'

He arrived breathlessly at the stage door entrance and was stopped by the doorman. 'Who are you?' asked the doorman.

'I'm "Hark, I hear the cannons roar".'

'You're "Hark, I hear the cannons roar"? You're late, get up to make-up straight away.'

So he ran up to make-up. 'Who are you?' asked the make-up girl.

'I'm "Hark, I hear the cannons roar".'

'You're "Hark, I hear the cannons roar?" You're late, sit down here.' Then, she swiftly applied the make-up before telling him, 'Now, quick, get down to the stage, you're about to go on.'

So he dashed down to the stage.

'Who are you?' asked the stage manager.

'I'm "Hark, I hear the cannons roar".'

'You're "Hark, I hear the cannons roar"? Get on there, the curtain's about to go up!'

So he ran on to the stage. The curtain rose and the house was full. Suddenly there was an almighty bang behind him and the actor shouted, 'What the hell was that?!'

SPORT

BASEBALL

A horse visited a baseball stadium, trotted over to the manager and asked for a tryout. Impressed by the talking horse, the manager agreed.

The horse took batting practice and slammed several pitches out of the park. Next came fielding practice, and he stopped everything at shortstop, firing the ball to first base each time with amazing accuracy.

'That's unbelievable!' said the manager. 'Now let's see you run.'

The horse said, 'Are you kidding? If I could run, I wouldn't be trying out for your lousy baseball team!'

Arriving home from his Little League game, Billy swung open the front door excitedly.

'So, how did you do son?' asked his father, who had been unable to attend the game.

'You won't believe it!" said Billy. 'I was responsible for the winning run!'

'Really? How'd you do that?'

'I dropped the ball.'

BOXING

Manager: How would you like to fight for the crown?

Boxer: Great. I think I can take the queen in about three rounds.

'Just think,' said the boxer to his manager, 'tonight I'll be fighting on TV before millions of people.'

'Yes,' replied his manager, 'and they'll all know the result of the fight at least ten seconds before you do.'

Why will there never be women's boxing?

 – A woman wouldn't dream of putting on gloves without a purse and shoes to match.

CRICKET

Two aliens were visiting Earth to research local customs. They split up so that they could learn more in the time allowed, and one happened to stumble across a game of cricket but mistook it for a strange religious ceremony. Afterwards, he met up with his fellow alien and described what he had seen.

'I went to a large green field shaped like a meteorite crater. Around the edges, several hundred worshippers gathered. Then two priests walk to the centre of the field to a rectangular area and hammer six spears into the ground, three at each end. Then eleven more priests walk out, clad in white robes. Then two high priests wielding clubs walk to the centre and one of the other priests starts throwing a red orb at the ones with the clubs.'

'Incredible!' said the other alien. 'What happens next?'

'Then it begins to rain.'

DARTS

Two men were competing in a national darts event. The second player was left with 100 to win. His first dart went in the treble twenty and his second dart was a single twenty, leaving him double ten for the match. He took careful aim but his final throw hit the wire and rebounded point-first into the head of a nun who was sitting in the front row, killing her instantly.

The match announcer boomed out the score: 'One nun dead and eighty.'

GOLF

Two friends were recounting their most recent dreams.

'I dreamed I was on holiday,' said one, 'and I was playing golf in this beautiful setting. The sun was shining brightly, the birds were singing and the waves were lapping on the nearby beach. It was idyllic. What a golf course! What a dream!'

'I had a great dream, too,' recalled the other. 'I dreamed I was on a date with two gorgeous women and having the time of my life.'

'Hey!' cried his friend, hurt. 'You dreamed you were with two gorgeous women, and you didn't call me?'

'I did, but your wife said you'd gone off to play golf.'

A wife was becoming concerned because her husband was more than four hours late returning home after his regular Saturday afternoon game of golf. When he finally pulled into the driveway, she rushed out to greet him.

'Where have you been?' she asked.

'Andy had a heart attack on the fourth hole,' he replied.

'Oh, that's terrible.'

'I know. All day long it was hit the ball, drag Andy, hit the ball, drag Andy...'

A golfer's round got off to an inauspicious start. His tee shot on the first hole sailed out of bounds and across a road, his fifth shot ended up in a stream, and his seventh landed in the woods. In total, he lost three brand-new golf balls on that hole.

Driving at the second hole, he hooked his drive wildly on to an adjoining railway track. 'Damn!' he cursed. 'There goes another new ball!' His next shot fared no better, flying into a corn field. 'That's yet another new ball I've lost!' he groaned. 'This round is costing me a fortune!'

Watching his struggles, a player in the group behind suggested, 'In view of the number of balls you lose, why don't you play with an old ball?'

'Because,' replied the hack golfer sourly, 'I've never had one!'

An octogenarian who was an avid golfer moved to a new town and joined the local country club. On his first visit to the club, he was unable to find a partner but was so keen to play that the assistant professional took pity on him and said he would accompany him around the course.

'To make it fair,' said the assistant pro, 'I'll give you a sixteen handicap.'

'I really don't need a handicap,' said the old man, 'as I have been playing quite well. The only real problem I have is getting out of sand traps.' The pair set off, and the old man proved himself a highly competent player. Then at the fourteenth hole, his drive landed in one of the sand traps around the hole. Taking his sand wedge, he lofted the ball on to the green and watched it roll into the hole.

The assistant pro walked over to the sand trap where his opponent was still standing and said, 'Great shot, but I thought you said you have a problem getting out of sand traps?'

'I do,' said the old man, extending his arm. 'Please, give me a hand.'

A husband and wife were out playing golf when, on the tenth hole, the man found himself in the rough with a barn between himself and the green. As he pondered how he was going to save par, his wife suggested, 'Why not open the front and rear barn doors and hit through the barn?'

After careful consideration, he decided to give it a try. So he opened the doors and hit a low shot, which smacked off the barn door and rebounded to hit his wife right between the eyes, killing her instantly.

Six weeks later, he was finally ready to start playing golf again. The first time out on the course with a work colleague, he somehow found himself in the same predicament on the tenth hole: right behind the barn. He couldn't believe it. Considering the shot, his workmate suggested, 'Why not open the barn doors and hit right through it?'

'No way!' replied the man. 'I tried that a few weeks ago and made a triple bogey.'

Jim was unlucky by nature. He loved betting on the horses but they repeatedly let him down. He dabbled in the stock market but always backed losers. Even his wife ran off with his best friend. Throughout this catalogue of misfortune, the one constant in Jim's life was golf. He wasn't very good – only occasionally breaking 100 – but every weekend, whatever the weather, he was out on the course.

Then one day, he was taken ill and died. In accordance with his wishes, he was cremated and his ashes were to be scattered just off the fairway on the twelfth hole of his local course.

A small gathering of friends turned up at the twelfth to witness the ceremony. It was a beautiful, sunny day but then just as the ashes were being strewn, a sudden gust of wind sprang up and blew Jim out of bounds.

A group of four watched a lone golfer play up short of the green they were on. As they moved on to the next tee, they saw him hurriedly chip on to the green and putt out. He then ran to the tee where they were about to drive off.

'Excuse me,' he said breathlessly. 'Would you mind if I played through? I've just heard that my wife has been involved in a terrible accident.'

A man went on a week's golfing holiday. On his first day, he caught up with an attractive lady golfer on the fourth hole and suggested that they play the rest of the round together. She agreed, and to make things interesting they had a small wager of ten dollars on the round. She proved to be an excellent golfer and won the bet. Captivated by her beauty, he offered her a lift home and kissed her goodbye.

The next day, he again spotted her on the course, and they renewed their competition. To his dismay, she defeated him once more, but his pain was eased when she allowed him to kiss her passionately on the way home.

This continued for the rest of the week. Each day, she narrowly beat him at golf – thereby denting his competitive male ego – but he enjoyed her company so much that he forgave her. Indeed, on their drive home on the Friday, he told her that he had booked them into a top-class restaurant followed by a night of passion in the penthouse suite of a five-star hotel. However, instead of being flattered, she suddenly burst into tears.

'I can't sleep with you,' she sobbed.

'Why not?' he asked. 'We've been getting on so well all week.'

'Because,' she said tearfully, 'I'm a transvestite.'

Hearing this bombshell, he swerved the car violently off the road, screeching to a halt on the grass verge.

'You lying cheating bastard!' he screamed.

'I'm so sorry…'

'You've been playing off the ladies' tee all week!'

Tom and Bill were playing golf when Tom sliced his shot into a deep wooded gully. Taking his eight-iron, he clambered down the embankment in search of his ball. After spending ten minutes hacking at the undergrowth, he suddenly spotted something glistening among the leaves. As he got closer, he could see that it was an eight-iron in the hands of a human skeleton.

Tom immediately called up, 'Hey, Bill, I've made a shocking discovery!'

'What is it?' shouted Bill.

'Bring me my wedge,' yelled Tom. 'There's no way you can get out of here with an eight-iron.'

A wife asked her husband, 'Why don't you play golf with Bob any more?'

The husband said, 'Would you play with someone who stands on his opponent's ball, cheats when he is in the bunker and deliberately puts down the wrong score on his card?'

'No.'

'Neither will Bob.'

🐕

A golfer spent an eternity over his tee shot. He kept measuring the wind strength and direction, checking the distance and practising his swing. Eventually, his playing partner became so impatient that he said, 'Come on! Get on with it! Just hit the damn ball!'

'You don't understand. My wife is watching me from the clubhouse balcony. I want to make this a perfect shot.'

'Forget it! You'll never hit her from here!'

Ted was quite a good golfer but he always had a problem with the eighth hole on his local course. It was a short par-3 but there was a large lake between the tee and the green, and Ted would invariably drive his ball into the water. It reached the point where he dreaded playing that hole because he knew he would end up in the lake. Eventually, one of his regular playing partners suggested Ted consult a therapist to rid him of his phobia.

So, Ted booked six sessions with the therapist who, through hypnosis, was able to plant thoughts in his mind. The idea was that whenever Ted stood on the eighth tee, he would not see the lake ahead, but instead a plush velvet fairway leading all the way down to the green.

Two months later, a group of golfers were sitting in the clubhouse when one said, 'I haven't seen Ted around lately.'

Another replied, 'Didn't you know? He drowned at the eighth six weeks ago.'

SKYDIVING

A man went skydiving. After a fantastic free fall, he pulled the ripcord to open his parachute but nothing happened. He tried everything, but couldn't get it to open. As he descended at speed, another man passed him going up.

The skydiver yelled, 'Hey, you know anything about parachutes?'

The other man shouted back, 'No. You know anything about gas cookers?'

SOCCER

The insects challenged the animals to a game of football, but unsurprisingly the animals were too strong for them and led 6–0 at half-time with two goals from the elephant, two from the rhinoceros and one each from the bear and the giraffe.

Things were no better in the second half and with just twenty minutes left the insects were trailing by nine goals. Then suddenly the centipede came on and began running rings around the animals, scoring goal after goal. The animals had no answer to him, and at the final whistle the insects had won 10–9.

As the jubilant insects applauded the centipede off the

pitch, the disconsolate elephant asked the fly, 'Why didn't you bring the centipede on earlier?'

The fly said, 'He was putting his boots on.'

TENNIS

A woman bought a tennis racket as a present for her son but when he tried it out the strings were too tight. So she took it back to the shop to have it restrung. Three days later, the racket was delivered back to her house but to her horror she saw that all the strings had been removed. It was nothing but the frame.

So she went back to the shop to complain. 'That tennis racket I bought the other day. Now it's got no strings! Why have you taken them all out?'

'Well, madam,' explained the shop manager, 'you see, we operate on a no-returns basis.'

TRANSPORT

A man walked into a car showroom and said to the salesman, 'My wife would like to talk to you about the Vauxhall Nova in the window.'

The salesman looked puzzled. 'We don't have a Vauxhall Nova in the window.'

The man said, 'You do now!'

A pilot and co-pilot were descending in readiness to make an emergency landing at an airport which they had never been to before. Suddenly the pilot looked out of the airplane windshield and exclaimed, 'Look how short the runway is! I've never seen one that short before!'

The co-pilot looked out and agreed. 'Wow, you're right! Are you sure we can make it?'

'We better had,' said the pilot, 'because we're almost out of fuel.'

Trying not to betray his nerves, he went on the intercom and told the passengers to put their heads between their knees and prepare for an emergency landing. Then he set the flaps to full down and slowed the plane to a little over stall speed. The huge jumbo jet came screaming in to land, barely under control. The pilot was sweating profusely while the co-pilot said a silent prayer. After what seemed a lifetime, they finally managed to touch down and came screeching to a halt just yards from the far edge of the runway, tyres smoking.

'My God! That was close!' gasped the pilot, mopping the sweat from his brow. 'That runway was unbelievably short!'

'Yeah!' said the co-pilot, 'and so wide, too!

Why did the man call his car 'baby'?
  – Because it never went out without a rattle.

What do you write on the headstone of a dead car?
  - Rust In Peace.

A magician was working on a cruise ship in the Caribbean. As the audience was different each week, the magician performed the same tricks over and over again. The only problem was that the captain's parrot witnessed the routine every week and soon worked out the secrets of the act. Before long, the bird started shouting out in the middle of the act, 'It's up his sleeve,' 'There's a secret compartment,' and 'All the cards are the eight of diamonds.' The magician was furious but could do nothing because the parrot was the captain's favourite bird.

Then one day, the ship collided with a rock and sank. The magician found himself clinging to a large piece of wood in the middle of the ocean, and when he looked up there was the parrot. For days, they glared at each other in silence until finally the parrot squawked, 'OK, I give up. Where's the ship?'

A man told his friend, 'My brother tried to make a new kind of car. He took the engine from a Mercedes, the transmission from a BMW, the wheels from a Ford and the exhaust from a Vauxhall.'

'What did he get?'

'Five years.'

Genuine Statements Made on Car Insurance Claims Forms

• As I reached an intersection a hedge sprang up obscuring my vision and I did not see the other car.

• The accident happened because I had one eye on the lorry in front, one eye on the pedestrian and the other on the car behind.

• In an attempt to kill a fly, I drove into a telephone pole.

• When I saw I could not avoid a collision I stepped on the gas and crashed into the other car.

• I pulled into a lay-by with smoke coming from under the hood. I realized the car was on fire so took my dog and smothered it with a blanket.

• The other car collided with mine without giving warning of its intention.

• The accident happened when the right front door of a car came round the corner without giving a signal.

• I started to slow down but the traffic was more stationary than I thought.

• I told the police that I was not injured, but on removing my hat found that I had a fractured skull.

• I didn't think the speed limit applied after midnight.

• The guy was all over the road. I had to swerve a number of times before I hit him.

A woman was driving along the highway at eighty miles an hour when she noticed a motorcycle policeman following her. Instead of slowing down, she picked up speed to ninety miles an hour. When she looked back again, there were two motorcycles following her. She put her foot on the gas and sped up to ninety-five. The next time she glanced back, there were three cops following her.

Suddenly she spotted a gas station looming ahead. She screeched to a stop and ran into the ladies' room. Ten minutes later, she innocently walked out. The three cops were standing there waiting for her. Without batting an eye, she said coyly, 'I'll bet none of you thought I would make it.'

A river pilot was guiding a ship up an estuary when suddenly the vessel ran aground. The captain yelled at him, 'Tony said you knew every sandbank in this river!'

'I do,' replied the pilot. 'And that was one of them.'

A woman queued for over an hour to get her driving licence renewed. When she saw her photo, she complained to the clerk, 'I was standing in line for so long that I look rather angry in this picture. It's not a good likeness.'

'Don't worry about it,' said the clerk. 'If the cops pull you over, that's how you're going to look anyway.'

A man was shaving in the bathroom when his wife suddenly ran in, screaming, 'Someone's just driven off in our car!'

'Did you try to stop him?' asked the husband.

'No,' she said, 'but I did get the licence plate number.'

Why did the man drive his car into the lake?
  - He wanted to dip his headlights.

How many angels can fit in a Honda?

– All of them. For it is written: 'All of my angels shall sing my praises in one Accord.'

A man was crossing the road when he was hit by a car, which then sped off. A police officer asked the injured man, 'Did you get a look at the driver?'

'No,' he said, 'but I can tell you it was my ex-wife.'

'How do you know?' asked the officer.

'I'd recognize her laugh anywhere.'

A car mechanic received a repair order that read: 'Check for clunking sound when going around corners.'

So he took the car out for a test drive, made a right turn and heard a clunk. He then made a left turn and again heard a clunk. Back at the shop, he opened the car's trunk and immediately discovered the problem. He duly returned the repair order to the service manager with the note: 'Remove bowling ball from trunk.'

How to Identify Where a Driver is From
- One hand on wheel, one hand on horn: Chicago
- One hand on wheel, one finger out window: New York
- One hand on wheel, one hand on newspaper, foot solidly on accelerator: Boston
- One hand on wheel, cradling cell phone, brick on accelerator: California.
- Both hands on wheel, eyes shut, both feet on brake, quivering in terror: Ohio, but driving in California
- Both hands in air, gesturing, both feet on accelerator, head turned to talk to someone in back seat: Italy
- One hand on latte, one knee on wheel, cradling cell phone, foot on brake, mind on game: Seattle
- One hand on wheel, one hand on hunting rifle, alternating between both feet being on the accelerator and both on the brake, throwing a McDonalds bag out of the window: Texas male
- One hand constantly refocusing the rear-view mirror to show different angles of big hair, one hand going between mousse, brush and rattail to keep the helmet hair going, both feet on the accelerator, poodle steering the car, chrome .38 revolver with mother-of-pearl inlaid handle in the glove compartment: Texas female
- Four-wheel-drive pickup truck, shotgun mounted in rear window, beer cans on floor, squirrel tails attached to antenna, cousin/spouse in passenger seat: Arkansas

• Two hands gripping wheel, blue hair barely visible above window level, driving at thirty-five miles an hour on the interstate in the left lane with the left blinker on: Florida.

A driver was speeding along the highway, safe in the knowledge that all the cars around him were also speeding. However, as they passed a speed camera, he was caught and pulled over.

As the traffic cop wrote out the ticket, the driver protested, 'I know I was exceeding the speed limit, but all the other cars around me were going just as fast. I don't think it's fair that I've been singled out.'

The traffic cop looked at him and asked, 'Ever been fishing?'

'Yeah,' said the driver, puzzled.

The cop grinned. 'Did you ever catch all the fish?'

A husband and wife went to the check-in desk of a budget airline.

'Do you have reservations?' asked the check-in clerk.

'Of course we have reservations,' said the husband, 'but we're flying with you anyway.'

A Mini pulled alongside a Rolls-Royce at the traffic lights. 'Do you have a built-in satnav?' its driver asked the man in the Rolls.

'Of course I do,' was the haughty reply.

'Do you have a back-seat DVD player?'

The Rolls driver sighed. 'I have that, too.'

'Do you have a double bed in the back?' the Mini driver wanted to know.

Ashen-faced, the Rolls driver sped off.

That afternoon, he had a mechanic install a double bed in his car. A week later, the Rolls driver passed the same Mini, parked on the side of the road with its back windows fogged up and steam pouring out. The arrogant driver pulled over, got out of the Rolls and banged on the Mini's rear window.

'I just want you to know that I've had a double bed installed,' announced the Rolls driver loftily.

The Mini driver rolled his window down and frowned at the Rolls driver. 'You got me out of the shower to tell me that?'

A businessman was at the airport waiting for his flight when he realized he had forgotten his watch. Seeing a guy walking past carrying two suitcases, he asked him for the time.

'Sure. Which country?' said the guy, looking at his watch.

'How many countries have you got?' asked the businessman.

'All the countries in the world.'

'That's a pretty cool watch you've got there,' said the businessman, impressed.

'You ain't seen nothing yet. This watch also has a GPS facility, music player, the Internet, and TV displayed on a miniature colour screen.'

'That's amazing! I wish I had a watch like that. I don't suppose you'd consider selling it?'

'As a matter of fact the novelty has started to wear off, so for eight hundred dollars you can have it.'

The businessman got out his cheque book and excitedly wrote a cheque for eight hundred dollars. The seller then took off the watch and handed it over.

'Congratulations. Here is your new hi-tech watch,' he said. He then handed the businessman the two suitcases. 'And here are the batteries.'

VACATION AND LEISURE

A Latin American tour guide was addressing a party of seniors about the country they were visiting. At the end of the tour, he asked if there were any questions.

One man asked, 'What's the number one sport in this country?'

'Bullfighting,' replied the guide.

'Isn't that revolting?'

'No,' said the guide. 'That's number two.'

While trekking through the prehistoric jungle, an explorer found a huge dead dinosaur with a pigmy standing beside it. The explorer asked incredulously, 'Did you kill that?'

'Yes,' said the pigmy.

'How the hell did a little guy like you manage to kill a beast like that?'

'With my club,' replied the pigmy.

Amazed, the explorer asked, 'How big is your club?'

The pigmy said, 'There's about fifty of us.'

A man was getting a haircut before going on holiday to Rome. He mentioned the trip to the barber, who was less than impressed.

'What's so good about Rome?' asked the barber. 'Why do you want to go there? It's crowded, dirty and full of Italians. You're crazy to go to Rome. So how are you getting there?'

'We're taking American Airlines,' the man replied. 'We got a great rate.'

'American Airlines?' the barber scoffed. 'That's a terrible airline. Their planes are old, their flight attendants are useless and their flights are always delayed. So, where are you staying in Rome?'

'At the Golden Garden Hotel.'

'That dump! That's the worst hotel in the city. The rooms are small, the service is surly and they're over-priced. So, what will you be doing when you get there?'

'We're going to go to tour the Vatican and we hope to see the Pope.'

'You'll be lucky!' laughed the barber. 'You and a million other people trying to see him. He'll look the size of an ant. Good luck on this lousy trip of yours! You're going to need it.'

A month later, the man again came in for his regular haircut. The barber asked him about his trip to Rome.

'It was wonderful,' explained the man. 'Not only were we on one of American Airlines' brand-new planes, but it was overbooked and they bumped us up to first class. The food and wine were wonderful, and the stewardesses were very attentive and helpful. The flight was bang on time, so we didn't miss a minute of our trip. The hotel was great, they'd just finished a twenty-million-dollar refurbishment and now it's the finest hotel in the city. They, too, were overbooked, so they apologized and gave us the presidential suite at no extra charge!'

'Huh,' muttered the barber. 'I bet you didn't get to see the Pope!'

'Actually, we were lucky, for as we toured the Vatican a Swiss Guard tapped me on the shoulder and explained that the Pope likes to meet some of the visitors in person.

He took me to a private room and sure enough, five minutes later the Pope walked through the door and shook my hand! I knelt down as he spoke a few words to me.'

'Really?' asked the barber. 'What did he say?'

'He said, "Where did you get that lousy haircut?"'

Two hunters went moose hunting every winter but without success. Finally, they devised what seemed a foolproof plan – they acquired an authentic moose costume and learned to imitate the call of a female moose. The plan was to hide in the costume, attract the male moose, and when he got close enough they would jump out of the costume and shoot him.

So they found a suitable clearing, climbed into the costume and began giving the moose love call. Sure enough, a few minutes later a huge bull burst out of the forest and into the clearing. When the bull was within range, the guy in the front of the costume said, 'Right, now let's get out and shoot him.'

But after struggling desperately for what seemed like an age, the guy in the back cried, 'The zip is stuck! We can't get out! What are we going to do?'

'Well,' said the guy in the front, 'I'm going to start nibbling grass, but you'd better brace yourself.'

Three holidaymakers who became lost in the jungle were captured by cannibals. The cannibal king told the prisoners that they could live if they passed a trial. The first step of the trial was to go to the forest and get ten pieces of the same kind of fruit.

So all three men went their separate ways to gather fruits. The first one came back and said to the king, 'I've brought ten apples.'

The king then explained the trial to him. 'You have to shove the fruits up your butt without any expression on your face or you'll be eaten.'

The first apple went in, but on the second one the man winced in pain, so he was killed.

The second man arrived and showed the king ten berries. When the king explained the trial to the man he thought it would be easy, but on the ninth berry he burst out laughing and was killed.

The first guy and the second guy met in Heaven. The first one asked, 'Why did you laugh? You almost got away with it!'

The second one replied, 'I couldn't help it. I saw the third guy coming with pineapples.'

An Australian guy went into a Spanish bar where Jill the barmaid immediately noticed his accent. They started chatting and at the end of the evening he asked her if she wanted to have sex. Although attracted to him, she said no, but he then offered to pay her two hundred dollars to sleep with him. Since she was travelling the world and was running short of money, she relented.

The next night, the same guy again turned up at the bar and showed Jill plenty of attention. At the end of the evening, he asked her if she would sleep with him again for two hundred dollars. As the previous time had been great, she agreed.

This went on for five nights in total, but on the sixth night the guy walked into the bar, ordered a beer and just sat quietly in the corner. Jill was disappointed and eventually went over to talk to him. She asked him whereabouts in Australia he was from.

'Brisbane,' he replied.

'Me, too,' she said. 'What suburb?'

'Oxley.'

'That's amazing!' she said. 'So am I. What street?'

'Hill Street.'

'Incredible! Me, too! What number?'

'Twenty-six,' he said.

'I don't believe this!' she gasped. 'I'm from number twenty-eight. In fact, my parents still live there.'

'I know,' he said. 'Your father gave me one thousand dollars to give to you.'

Before going on vacation, a man phoned a seaside hotel to check on its exact location. The proprietor said, 'It's only a stone's throw from the beach.'

'How will I recognize it?' asked the man.

'Easy,' said the proprietor. 'It's the one with all the broken windows.'

A middle-aged married couple were members of a touring party that went snorkelling in the Caribbean. After spending an hour in the water, everyone got back on the boat except for the wife and a handsome young man. As she continued to explore underwater, she noticed that wherever she swam, he did, too. She continued snorkelling for another thirty minutes, and so did he.

She felt flattered by his attention, and as she took off her fins she coyly asked him why he had remained in the water for so long.

'I couldn't get out until you did,' he replied matter-of-factly. 'I'm the lifeguard.'

An American tourist in Africa was admiring a necklace worn by a local tribesman. 'What is it made of?' she asked.

'Crocodile's teeth,' replied the tribesman.

'I guess,' said the tourist, 'that they mean as much to you as pearls do to us?'

'Not exactly,' said the tribesman. 'Anyone can open an oyster.'

A group of friends went deer hunting and paired off for the day. That night, one of the hunters returned alone, staggering under the weight of a mighty stag with impressive antlers.

'Where's Henry?' asked the others.

'Oh, he had some sort of attack. He's a couple of miles back up the trail.'

'You mean you left Henry lying out there and carried the deer back!?'

'It was a tough call,' admitted the hunter, 'but I figured no one is going to steal Henry.'

After an exhausting ten-hour drive to their holiday hotel, a newlywed couple decided to cool down with a swim in the hotel pool. The wife had obviously shed a few pounds through pre-wedding jitters, because each time she dived into the pool she either lost the top or bottom of her skimpy new bikini. But since they had the pool to themselves, they just laughed and retrieved the pieces. Later, they dressed for dinner and went down to the hotel restaurant. While waiting for a table, they sat in the lounge and ordered drinks. Above the bar was a huge, empty, glistening fish tank. Curious, the husband asked, 'Why is such a beautiful fish tank empty?'

The barman grinned knowingly as he replied, 'That's not a fish tank, sir. It's the swimming pool.'

Before setting off on an expedition to the Amazon rainforest, a solo traveller consulted a survival expert who advised him on what he should take in the event of an emergency. The expert said, 'The most important things to remember are food, matches, distress flares, a compass, a canteen of water and a deck of playing cards.'

The traveller looked puzzled. He said, 'I understand that the compass and distress flares are essential if you get lost, but what use is a deck of playing cards?'

'Well, you know how it is,' said the survival expert. 'As soon as you start playing solitaire, someone is bound to come up behind you and say, "Put that red three on top of the black four."'

Two mountaineers reached a deep fissure in a glacier. 'Careful,' said one. 'My mountain guide fell down there last year.'

'I bet you feel bad about that,' said the other.

'Not really. It was pretty old and missing a few pages.'

A party of wealthy American tourists were travelling by coach through the Australian outback when they stopped at a bridge. On the riverbank below, a man was trapped in the jaws of a crocodile, already half devoured so that only his head and upper torso were visible.

One tourist turned to her neighbour and said, 'I thought the people in these parts were supposed to be poor, Eleanor, but that guy's got a Lacoste sleeping bag!'

Mike and his girlfriend Alice lived in Texas, but Mike had always wanted to see the amazing natural sky illumination known as the northern lights. Alice was less enthusiastic but decided that a few days in Canada would at least be a nice break from Houston.

So they drove all the way up to Canada. By the time they arrived, Mike was beside himself with excitement. The northern lights were fantastic – the greatest light show he had ever seen, the whole sky ablaze with colour. He jumped out of the car and took in the wonder of it all, but his girlfriend stayed in the vehicle reading a magazine. He couldn't believe her lack of interest. So eventually, he went over to her and said, 'What's the matter? Does the aurora bore ya, Alice?'

WORKING LIFE

It was the postman's last day at work after thirty-five years of delivering the mail in all kinds of weather to the same neighbourhood. At each of the houses along his route that day he was presented with a token of appreciation by his grateful customers. Laden with gifts of cigars, chocolates and wine, he arrived at the final house on his route where he was met by a woman in a revealing negligee. She took him silently by the hand, led him upstairs and had wild sex with him in the bedroom.

Afterwards, they went downstairs where she prepared him a sumptuous breakfast of sausages, bacon, eggs, mushrooms, tomatoes, fried potatoes and freshly squeezed orange juice. Finally, she poured him a cup of steaming coffee but as she did so, he noticed a dollar bill under the cup.

'That was simply amazing,' he said, 'but tell me, what's with the dollar bill?'

'Oh,' she explained. 'Last night, I told my husband that today would be your last round and that we should do something special for you. I asked him what to give you. He said, "Screw him, give him a dollar." But the breakfast was my idea.'

One evening, two social workers were walking through a rough part of town when they saw a man lying semi-conscious on the pavement in a pool of blood.

'Help me,' wailed the man, 'I've been beaten up and robbed.'

As they stepped over the body and continued on their way, one social worker turned to the other and said, 'You know, whoever did that really needs help.'

Jim went for a job on a building site. The foreman asked him, 'Can you make tea?'

'Yes,' said Jim.

'Can you drive a forklift?'

'Bloody hell!' exclaimed Jim. 'How big is the teapot?!'

Boss: 'Is everything OK in the office?'

Employee: 'Yes, it's all under control. It's been a very busy day; I haven't stopped.'

Boss: 'Can you do me a favour?'

Employee: 'Sure. What is it?'

Boss: 'Hurry up and take your shot. I'm behind you on the eleventh hole.'

Jerry was so excited about his promotion to vice president of the company he worked for that he kept bragging about it to his wife for weeks on end. Finally, she could take no more and told him bluntly, 'Listen, it means nothing, they even have a vice president of peas at the grocery store!' His pride dented by the revelation, he decided to check whether her claim was really true or whether it was something she had just invented to prick his pomposity. So he called the grocery store and said, 'May I speak to the vice president of peas... assuming there is such a person?' The voice at the other end replied, 'Canned or frozen?'

A wife suspected that her husband was having an affair with his pretty young PA, so one day she decided to try to catch him out by calling in at his office unannounced. Sure enough, she walked in to find the PA sitting on the husband's lap.

Without hesitating, he dictated, '… and in conclusion, gentlemen, regardless of shortages, I cannot continue to operate this office with just one chair.'

A situations vacant advertisement was placed in an office window. It read: 'HELP WANTED. Must be able to type, have computer skills and be bilingual. We are an equal opportunity employer.'

A dog saw the advert and went inside. When the dog wagged his tail and put his paw on the sign, the receptionist realized that he had come about the job and fetched the office manager. The manager took one look at the dog and said, 'I'm sorry but I can't hire you. The advert says you have to be able to type.'

Hearing this, the dog jumped on to a chair, typed out a perfect letter and handed it to the manager. Although impressed, the manager said, 'But the advert says you must have computer skills.'

The dog then went over to the computer and created an immaculate spreadsheet. The manager was amazed. 'Look,' he said, 'you're obviously an extremely intelligent dog, but I still can't give you the job.'

So the dog went over to the advert and pointed with his paw to the section about being an equal opportunity employer. 'Yes,' said the manager, 'but the advert also says you have to be bilingual.'

And the dog went, 'Miaow!'

Getting ready to start his new job, a young accountant spent a week with the retiring accountant that he was replacing. He hoped to pick up a few tips from the old master and studied his daily routine closely.

Every morning, the experienced accountant began the day by opening his desk drawer, taking out a frayed envelope and removing a yellowing piece of paper. He then read it, nodded his head sagely, returned the envelope to the drawer and started his day's work.

After the old man retired, the new boy could

hardly wait to read for himself the message in the drawer. Surely, the envelope must contain the secret to accounting success, a pearl of wisdom to be treasured for ever. The anticipation was so great that his hands were actually trembling as he opened the drawer and took out the mysterious envelope. And there, inside, on that aged piece of paper, he read the following message: 'Debits in the column nearest the potted plant; credits in the column towards the door.'

No sooner had a man arrived at the office for work than he started yawning.

'You look tired,' said a colleague.

'I know,' he said. 'I don't get enough sleep. You see, my wife is afraid of burglars, so she used to wake me up every time she heard a noise in the night. But then I told her that burglars don't make a noise. So now she wakes me up every time she doesn't hear a noise!'

As part of its equal opportunities policy, an international company hired several cannibals. 'You're all part of our team now,' said the HR rep during the welcoming briefing. 'You get all the usual benefits and you can go to the cafeteria for something to eat, but please don't eat any of the other employees.' The cannibals promised they wouldn't.

A month later their boss remarked, 'You're all working very hard, and I'm satisfied with you. However, one of our secretaries has disappeared. Do any of you know what happened to her?' The cannibals all shook their heads.

After the boss had left, the leader of the cannibals said to the others, 'Which one of you idiots ate the secretary?'

A hand rose hesitantly. The cannibal leader roared, 'You idiot! For a month we've been eating managers and nobody noticed anything, but no, you had to go and eat someone who actually does something!'

A team of archaeologists were excavating in Israel when they found a cave. Written across a wall of the cave were the following symbols in this order: a woman, a donkey, a shovel, a fish and a Star of David.

The archaeologists decided that the markings dated back at least three thousand years and spent months studying them before announcing their conclusions at a conference in front of a packed audience.

At the conference, the team leader stood up and, pointing at the first drawing, said, 'The presence of a woman shows that these people were family oriented and held women in high esteem. They were clearly intelligent as the donkey symbol indicates that they had learned to use animals to help till the soil. The next drawing looks like a shovel, suggesting that they had made tools to help them in their work. Further proof of their intelligence is the fish symbol, showing that if famine had hit the land, they had the ability to trawl the sea for food. The last symbol appears to be the Star of David, which means they were obviously Hebrews.'

The audience applauded enthusiastically, but then a little old Jewish man stood up at the back of the room and said, 'You're all idiots! Hebrew is read from right to left! The inscription says: "Holy mackerel, dig the ass on that woman!"'

A man was given the job of painting white lines down the middle of a road. On the first day he painted six miles, on the second day he painted three miles, but on the third day he painted less than a mile.

'Why are you painting less each day?' asked the foreman.

'I can't help it,' said the workman. 'Each day I get farther away from the tin of paint.'

Employer Speak

Competitive salary: we remain competitive by paying less than our competitors.

Fast-paced company: we have no time to train you.

Some overtime required: some time every night and some time every weekend.

Flexible hours: work 40 hours, get paid for 25.

Duties will vary: anyone in the office can boss you around.

Profit-sharing plan: once it's shared among the higher-ups, there won't be a profit.

The successful applicant will need to be motivated: we're paying you peanuts.

Must have an eye for detail: we have no quality control.

Problem-solving skills essential: the company is in chaos.

Requires team leadership skills: you'll have the responsibilities of a manager, without the pay or respect.

Competitive environment: high turnover of staff.

Career minded: female applicants must be childless and stay that way.

On his last day at work, the outgoing CEO of a large company handed his successor three numbered envelopes and suggested, 'Open these if you come up against a problem you can't solve.'

Six months later, sales were falling and the new CEO was under pressure. Remembering the advice, he reached into his drawer and opened envelope number one. The note inside read: 'Blame your predecessor.' So he quickly called a press conference, subtly laid the blame for the poor sales figures at the feet of the previous CEO, and company confidence was restored.

A year later, the company suffered another dip in sales. The CEO wasted no time in opening envelope number two. The message inside read: 'Reorganize.' So he restructured the company and things soon picked up.

But then after a run of profitable quarters, sales slumped again. The CEO headed straight for envelope number three. The message inside read: 'Prepare three envelopes.'

Two postmen had just finished their rounds when one saw the other deliberately stamp on a snail. 'Why did you step on that snail?' he asked.

'Because the damn thing's been following me around all day.'

A young man fresh out of business school answered a job vacancy ad for an accounting post with a small company.

The company boss said, 'I need someone with an accounting degree who can do my worrying for me.'

'In what way?' the young man asked.

'I worry about a lot of things,' said the boss, 'but I don't want to have to worry about money. Your job will be to take all the money worries off my back.'

'I see, and how much will you be paying me?'

'I'll start you off at eighty thousand.'

'Eighty thousand?!' said the young man. 'How can such a small business afford to pay a sum like that?'

'That,' said the boss, 'is your first worry.'

An accountant went to see his doctor because he was having trouble sleeping at night.

'Have you tried counting sheep?' suggested the doctor.

'That's the problem,' said the accountant. 'I make a mistake and then spend three hours trying to find it.'

What's the difference between an English actuary and a Sicilian actuary?

- An English actuary can tell you how many people are going to die next year; a Sicilian actuary can give you their names.

Tom kept getting up late in the morning and as a result he was always late for work. His boss was mad at him and threatened to fire him if he didn't do something about it.

So, Tom went to the doctor who gave him a pill and told him to take it last thing at night before he went to bed. After taking the pill, Tom slept really well and was even up before his alarm went off in the morning. He then had a leisurely breakfast and drove cheerfully to work.

'Boss,' he smiled, 'the pill I took actually worked!'

'Good,' said the boss. 'But where were you yesterday?'

A man was called into his manager's office for violating the dress code. The manager told him forcibly, 'You can't wear pyjamas for work!'

'But everyone else does,' he protested.

The manager sighed. 'That's because they're patients.'

One social worker asked a colleague, 'What time is it?'

'Sorry, I don't know. I don't have a watch.'

'Never mind,' said the first. 'The main thing is we talked about it.'

Two young engineers were chatting in the office. 'I saw you arrive on a brand-new bicycle this morning,' said one. 'Where did you get it?'

'Well,' said the other, 'it's a strange story. I was walking in the park yesterday evening when a shapely brunette pulled up, hopped off the bike, ripped off all her clothes and said, "Take what you want."'

The first engineer nodded. 'Good choice. The clothes probably wouldn't have fitted you.'

The manager of a latex manufacturing company was showing a young job seeker around the factory. First, the young man was shown the machine that made the teats for babies' feeding bottles. It went hiss, pop, hiss, pop – the hissing noise being the sound of the latex poured into the mould and the popping noise occurring as the hole was put into the end of the teat. Next, he was shown the machine that made condoms. It went hiss, hiss, hiss, pop.

'OK,' said the young man, trying to impress. 'I know that the hissing sound is the latex being poured into the mould. But what's the popping noise?'

The manager explained, 'We put a hole in every fourth condom we make.'

'Why do you do that?' asked the young man. 'It can't be very good for the condom industry.'

'No,' said the manager, 'but it's great for the baby bottle teat business!'

🐼

Successful Job Placement
Put the prospective employees in a room with only a table and two chairs. Leave them alone for two hours, without any instruction. At the end of that time, go back and see what they are doing.
• If they have taken the table apart in that time, put them in Engineering.
• If they are counting the butts in the ashtray, assign them to Finance.
• If they are screaming and waving their arms, send them off to Manufacturing.

- If they are talking to the chairs, mark them down for a job in Personnel.
- If they don't even look up when you enter the room, assign them to Security.
- If they try to tell you it's not as bad as it looks, send them to Marketing.
- If they are sleeping, they are clearly Management material.
- And if they've left early, put them in Sales.

Three insurance salesmen were boasting about their companies' speed of service.

The first said, 'When one of our policyholders died suddenly on Tuesday, we got the news that evening and were able to process the claim for the wife with such speed that she received the cheque by Friday morning.'

The second said, 'When one of our insured died on Tuesday, we were able to hand-deliver a cheque to his widow that same evening.'

The third said, 'I can beat that. Our office is on the tenth floor. One of our insured, who was washing a window on the thirtieth floor, slipped and fell on Tuesday. We handed him his cheque as he passed our floor!'

A powerfully built young man was boasting about his physique to his fellow construction workers. He claimed he could beat anyone on the building site in a trial of strength and took great delight in mocking one of the older workmen. Eventually, the older man became so irritated by the taunts that he issued a challenge to the cocky young upstart.

The older man said, 'I'll bet you a week's wages that I can haul something in a wheelbarrow over to that outbuilding that you won't be able to wheel back.'

'You're a weak old man!' laughed the youngster. 'I'd feel embarrassed taking the money off you. But if you don't mind losing a week's wages, off you go.'

With that, the older man grabbed the wheelbarrow by the handles. Then, nodding to the young man, he said, 'OK, get in.'

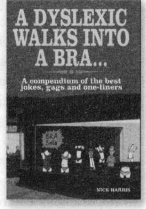